W9-BLZ-816

With clarity and a gracious spirit, Wittmer provides a resource that I can hand my parishioners who are seeking answers to the questions raised in Rob Bell's *Love Wins*.

—PASTOR DAVID BEELEN
Madison Square Church, Grand Rapids, MI

Christ Alone provides a clear assessment of Rob Bell's *Love Wins*. With skill and wit, Wittmer shows that in the end, God loves and wins only if he is truly and completely who he has revealed himself to be in both living and written Word.

—PASTOR JEFFREY D. HALSTED
Calvary Baptist Church, Grand Rapids, MI

Christ Alone deftly guides us in the art of listening to history and the text so that we might engage the conversation beyond the controversy. Not afraid to ask the questions, but ready to give an answer when there are answers to be given, Wittmer walks the line between mystery and revelation culminating in the cross and resurrection and the good news that love has already won.

—CHRISTOPHER R. BREWER
Founder and Director of Gospel through Shared Experience
and editor of *Art that Tells the Story*

Readers will appreciate the combination of respect, insight and conviction. Wittmer helps us to see that the Bible's message is not embarrassing but a compelling story that fits the reality of God›s holiness and the darkness of the human heart.

—PASTOR NATE ARCHER
Peace Church, Middleville, MI

Christ Alone is a gracious, respectful biblical and theological engagement with *Love Wins*. Wittmer's astute questions help readers discern the strengths and weaknesses of Rob Bell's positions.

—PROFESSOR DARWIN GLASSFORD
Calvin Theological Seminary

Wittmer's critique of *Love Wins* is fair, biblical, loving, and rooted in mainstream Christian thought. Readers learn or relearn biblical interpretations, biblical doctrines, teachings of historical church leaders, and an overall appreciation of who God is and what it means to live in the balance of God's grace and justice.

—PASTOR LEW VANDERMEER
New Community Church, Grand Rapids, MI

Christ Alone

Christ Alone

An Evangelical Response
to Rob Bell's *Love Wins*

Michael E. Wittmer

edenridge press

GRAND RAPIDS, MICHIGAN

Published by
Edenridge Press LLC
Grand Rapids, Michigan USA
service@edenridgepress.com

Quantity discount pricing is available.
service@edenridgepress.com
Fax: (616) 365-5797

ISBN-10 0982706332
ISBN-13 9780982706336

REL000000 Religion : General

Library of Congress Headings
1. Faith
2. Salvation—Christianity
3. Trust in God
I. Title

Contents

Preface

Hell has had a surprisingly prominent place in the popular imagination of cultures and religions around the world. In Christianity, too, writers and painters have produced speculative travelogues of the place of everlasting judgment. The biblical references are frightening enough, but in the vividly detailed imagery of Dante, Hieronymus Bosch, and Billy Sunday, there is a strange fascination with hell.

Hell has never functioned as a central dogma in historic Christianity. While acknowledging that everlasting punishment is clearly taught in Scripture, most Christians would say that it's not their favorite subject. Yet the reality of hell is one of those convictions that are inseparable from a wider web of beliefs. Not all rejections of hell follow the same logic, but they all challenge orthodox views concerning God's attributes, the person and work of Christ, and sin and redemption. And the version with the longest pedigree can be traced from Origen in the early third century to Schleiermacher (1768–1834) and his theological heirs. It's a trajectory best summarized in H.

Richard Niebuhr's classic description of Protestant liberalism: "A God without wrath brought men without sin into a kingdom without judgment through the ministrations of a Christ without a cross" (Niebuhr, 1959, p. 193).

Taking for granted that Christians today know the grammar, much less the logic, of Christian faith, we now have a generation that questions its premises and conclusions. It's neither pastorally responsible nor persuasive to dismiss these questions simply by invoking settled dogmas. We have to return to the Scriptures, examining the relevant passages for ourselves, in order to join the orthodox consensus as participants rather than mere spectators.

Rob Bell's *Love Wins* has sparked remarkable controversy. Of course, he's not the first evangelical to have challenged traditional Christian teaching on hell. Nevertheless, for a variety of reasons—not the least being his knack at popular communication—his book has attracted media hype as well as stern dismissals.

That's exactly why I'm delighted with Michael Wittmer's *Christ Alone: An Evangelical Response to Rob Bell's "Love Wins."* The current controversy will fade away as quickly as it burst on the scene, but the widespread doubts to which Bell gave voice are deeper and wider than we probably imagine. So in a sense, he gave us a wake-up call and Michael Wittmer has answered it. Although he engages with *Love Wins* directly, Wittmer's case is just as relevant for the many other expressions of Bell's thesis that we are sure to encounter in coming years.

Offering more light than heat, *Christ Alone* appreciates the attractiveness of Bell's questions and conclusions. Avoiding caricature and personal attack, he carefully evaluates Bell's interpretations of Scripture. It's not a careless diatribe against a book, but filled with pastoral wisdom for perennial questions. For example, he does not offer easy answers to the problem of evil: "Better to believe that God is all-powerful and all-loving and wrestle with evil than to weaken one aspect of God to make room for evil" (p. 14). Wittmer shares Bell's critique of "Platonized" versions of heaven. Yet here, as elsewhere, Wittmer points beyond false choices to a lush biblical landscape.

A close and sympathetic reader, Wittmer explains the senses in which Rob Bell's argument is and isn't universalist and how he follows Origen (emphasizing the human will) over Barth (emphasizing divine grace) in his account. Along the way, *Christ Alone* is peppered with thought-provoking statements. If Bell's account of God, sin, and salvation is accurate, then what makes the gospel surprising? Something more than what the average pagan already believes? Furthermore, "Why would a God who 'loves' enough to empty hell want to frighten people now with numerous warnings that sound like hell lasts forever?" (p. 22). Wouldn't that be a kind of sadistic deity, if in fact he has no intention of actually doing what he warns us about? Yet the chief insights of the book are found in Wittmer's careful and simple (though not simplistic) interpretation of the relevant passages in Scripture.

A good critique must be charitable as well as corrective. The views of others must be represented fairly, in terms that the other person would recognize as his or her own. Such opposing views must be stated in terms of what the proponent actually says, and not in terms of what one thinks they must say even thought they don't. Further, a good critique targets the actual content of the arguments that are public, not personal character and motives that remain hidden. Finally, a good critique not only tears down bad arguments, but builds a positive case. On all of these points, *Christ Alone* scores high marks, in my view. So let's avoid hand-wringing lamentations and follow Michael Wittmer's lead, making the most of the current controversy to deepen our own understanding of what we believe and why we believe it.

MICHAEL S. HORTON. PH.D.
J. Gresham Machen Professor of
Systematic Theology and Apologetics,
Westminster Seminary California

Introduction

I like Rob Bell. We've only spoken a few times—once about the themes in this book—but we know and genuinely appreciate each other. I have mostly followed his meteoric rise from a distance, learning about his next projects from friends and students who attend his church. I visited his church soon after it began, and I remember being impressed with how easily Rob connected with my generation. Many churches and pastors desperately want to be cool and relevant, and here was a preacher who didn't have to try. He just was. And people drove from far away to park on the grass and be a part of it.

I respect Rob Bell. He wrote *Love Wins* to start a dialogue about the most important issues of our faith, and this book is my attempt as an evangelical to join that conversation. I look forward to keeping the conversation going respectfully about both of our books, and inviting others to the table. In this book I will disagree, sometimes strongly, with the views presented in *Love Wins*. But my disagreement with Rob's ideas in no way diminishes my appreciation and respect for him as a person.

My respect for Rob Bell is the reason I refer to him by his last name throughout this book. That feels strange, because everyone who knows him simply calls him "Rob." And so did I when I wrote the first drafts of this manuscript. A few manuscript readers and my editor thought that using his first name might be taken as a sign of disrespect, so I agreed to follow normal publishing protocol and refer to him by his last name. Please don't take this as an attempt to "objectify" Rob or treat him as the "other." I only mean it as a sign of respect, and if it feels as weird to you as it does to me, then simply substitute the name "Rob" every time you read "Bell." From here on, that is what I will call him.

I do have significant concerns about some of the ideas expressed in *Love Wins*—not only about its views on hell, but also about the other doctrines which are inextricably connected with hell and the afterlife. Theology, or our understanding of God, is more like a sweater than a smorgasbord. We can't logically walk up to the Bible buffet and load up on the teachings we like while skipping the ones we don't: give me an extra helping of love but hold the stuff about wrath. Instead, our beliefs about God and the Christian life are intertwined like the strands of yarn in a cable-knit sweater. When we tug on one, the others tend to come, too.

And so it is with *Love Wins*. Rob Bell's *New York Times* best seller challenges what I take to be the traditional evangelical understanding of hell. But as I explain in this book, that scary topic (who *does* want to have to talk about hell?) is interwoven with other, even more foundational beliefs—including the good news itself. It's impossible to reassess the subject of hell without also reevaluating our beliefs about Scripture, God, sin, Jesus, the cross, and salvation. In the Bible, practically everything is interconnected with everything else. So in this book I will not only examine Bell's provocative statements on hell, but even more importantly, I will provide a serious and fair critique of his new vision for the Christian faith.

I have organized my book into themes, which generally follow the order of chapters in *Love Wins*. Occasionally I pull in related material from other chapters, but overall my chapters treat Bell's topics in the order in which he handles them. I cover the essential, foundational question of whether we can know about God and the afterlife, and if so, how much (chapters 1–2); how we should think about the afterlife—which is the focus of *Love Wins* (chapters 3–5); how our views of the afterlife influence more central beliefs about sin, the atonement, Jesus, and God (chapters 6–9); and finally, what practical difference any of this makes for understanding and proclaiming the gospel of Jesus Christ (chapter 10).

I have two main goals for you, the reader. First, I want to help you understand the biblical and theological issues, so whichever positions you eventually take, you'll at least be making informed decisions. I will help you understand these issues by responding biblically, theologically, and (I hope) fairly to the ideas in *Love Wins*. I examine Bell's use of Scripture, the implications of his arguments, and where he seems to fit historically as a theologian. Who else has expressed similar thoughts? Where do his ideas logically take you?

Second, I hope to persuade you to side with what the Scriptures and the church have historically said about these issues. Among its other subjects, *Love Wins* addresses the most important decision you'll ever make, and it's crucial that you understand your options. This critically important decision is whether or not to believe in Jesus Christ as Savior and Lord of your life. I hope that by reading this book you will gain a better understanding of who Jesus really is and why you should decide to follow him to eternal life. Jesus himself says he is the way, the truth, and the life. Even apart from the Bible, historians have documented that Jesus lived. The real question is whether he was crucified and resurrected as the very Son of God for the salvation of all of those who believe in him. I address that question head-on and invite you to consider the evidence just as millions have done for the last two thousand years. As I will explain, the traditional, evangelical story about God and salvation is the only story in which God truly loves, and it's also the only story in which he self-sacrificially wins.

Mystery

1

If your mind and heart are open, every question you'll ever ask about God will end in follow-up questions and deeper mystery. You may discover a satisfactory answer to your initial query, but that answer itself will generate a new question. Maybe you'll adequately answer that one, but sooner or later you'll be left to wonder.

Look, I'll show you.
"Is our world eternal or did it have a beginning?"
"It must have had a beginning."
"Then how did the world begin?
"God made it."
"Okay, then who made God?"

That was quick. Let's try another.
"Why is there evil in the world?"
"Because God gave us freedom."
"Why did he give us freedom?"

"Because without freedom we can't love."

"Alright, but why didn't God make us like the unfallen angels, with a freedom that always chooses love?"

"I don't know."

How easily we get stuck whenever we talk about God! If you ever think you have come to the end, if you dust off your hands and say, "That's it, I get it now, I have no further questions," then you can be sure, as Karl Barth said about the theological liberalism of Friedrich Schleiermacher, you've not been talking about God at all, but just about yourself in a really loud voice (see Torrance, p. 46).

Asking Big Questions

So Rob Bell rightly begins *Love Wins* with a series of big questions. Jesus is an immense God and the Bible is a spacious book, so there is bound to be a rather large remainder every time we do our theological division. And Bell wastes no time pointing out the leftover bits and pieces that don't easily fit into our tidy theological systems. Why would a loving God send anyone to hell forever? Why wouldn't God eventually soften up and save them?

And what determines who ends up in heaven or hell? Is it a special prayer we say, good works we do, or the kind of person we are? If the answer is what many churches have traditionally believed—that people escape hell and go to heaven by repenting of their sin and believing in Jesus—then is the difference an accident of birth? Most children born in West Michigan, where Bell's church is located and where I live, are privileged to grow up with a knowledge of Jesus, while Muslim children in the Middle East must wait for Christians to tell them the gospel. But what if the missionary's car has a flat tire? Will these Muslims go to hell because of a cheap tire?

And what if the missionary whose car makes it through is a Mormon, a Jehovah's Witness, or worse to some folks, a Republican? Their Jesus differs significantly from the orthodox Christian view. Will "converted" Muslims still go to hell for believing in the wrong Jesus?

The questions don't end for evangelicals like me who, despite our conservative voting records, remain reasonably confident that we believe in the real Jesus. What about our children who die before they are able to express their faith in our Lord? Many Christian parents take comfort in knowing that their deceased children had not yet reached the "age of accountability," when God begins to hold humans accountable for their moral choices. But as Bell observes (p. 4), such accountability language comes with its own set of problems. If it is true that all children who die before a certain age go to heaven, then why wouldn't loving parents kill their infants rather than risk losing them to eternal hell? Why wouldn't they sneak into Muslim countries and kill other people's children? Christians might coldly reason: "Sure, losing your child may hurt now, but we're actually doing you a favor, trading in this short life span so your child can live forever."

Perhaps this is why the so-called age of accountability is not expressly taught in Scripture. We have reason to think that God takes the children of believers to be with him, for the apostle Paul declares that the children of a believing parent "are holy" or special to him (1 Cor. 7:14). But God could not unequivocally tell us that all infants—or even all infants of Christian parents—automatically go to heaven without giving well-meaning parents a logical but terrible reason to destroy their own children. So we don't have an ironclad promise from God, and I suspect I know why. When our children die, we take comfort that they are holy to God, and we entrust them to the care of our Father, who loves them even more than we do.

My point is that Bell's big questions are not new. We all have pondered these problems at one time or another, and we are bound to do so again, whenever the events of our lives demand that we ask them. We are comforted by our prayer that our deceased child is alive with God, but we still wonder why God let our child pass away. One question seemingly solved. Another one raised. So it goes for all of us in this life of faith.

Asking Assertive Questions

Besides such enduring questions, however, Bell's opening chapter raises many questions that few evangelicals are struggling to answer. In my view, these additional questions don't drive us deeper into the mystery of God. Instead they seem to raise doubts about the evangelical view of salvation. Bell understands that his perspective on hell and salvation pushes the envelope in the evangelical world, and that many people will dismiss his ideas out of hand unless he gives them a compelling reason to stop and listen. So his first chapter attempts to shake readers—at least evangelical readers—out of their complacency by poking holes in their traditional view. If he can persuade us that our standard line, "Believe in the Lord Jesus, and you will be saved" (Acts 16:31), is a facile misreading of Scripture, then perhaps we'll be open to what he says about hell and salvation.

Bell's main strategy is to point out the many, seemingly different ways that people expressed their faith in the Bible. To use two of his examples (pp. 12–14), the thief on the cross asked Jesus, "Remember me when you come into your kingdom" (Luke 23:42), and Zacchaeus promised to "pay back four times the amount" he had stolen (Luke 19:8). But this doesn't mean that the thief was saved by what he said and Zacchaeus by what he planned to do. The thief's words and Zacchaeus's actions both sprung from the same act of regeneration. They were born again, and they expressed their new life in word and deed. It's not nearly as complicated as Bell makes it.

Bell pushes on, arguing that Jesus forgave the sins of a paralyzed man *because of the faith of his friends,* who lowered him through the ceiling to Jesus. Bell cites Mark 2:5—"When Jesus saw their faith, he said to the paralytic, 'Son, your sins are forgiven'"—and then asks if it's true that we can be saved by the faith of our friends (p. 15). A simple response is that the term "their" likely includes the paralytic himself, who at any rate was apparently in on the idea. It would be difficult to hoist a grown man onto the top of a house and through the roof if he didn't agree to be carried. If the paralyzed man didn't believe that Jesus could heal him, he simply wouldn't have been there. So while his friends demonstrated faith by their actions, the paralyzed man likely also had faith in Jesus, which is why Jesus responded to him with "Son, your sins are forgiven."

Bell's subsequent questions seem odd and off topic. He cites 1 Corinthians 7:15–16, which urges Christians to stay with their unbelieving spouse, for "How do you know, wife, whether you will save your husband? Or, how do you know, husband, whether you will save your wife?" Bell also notes that 1 Timothy 2:15 declares that "women will be saved through childbearing." Then he asks, Does salvation depend on "who you're married to, or whether you give birth to children?" (p.

15). I've spent my entire life in evangelical churches, and I haven't met anyone who thought that marriage or pregnancy might be their ticket to heaven. We know that Paul was not telling his readers to ride their spouse's or child's coattails into heaven, but simply exhorting them to resist the false teachers who disparaged marriage and childbearing.

Giving Incomplete Answers

Since Bell is explaining the way that Scripture says we are saved, I wonder why he didn't replace the obscure marriage and childbirth texts with the many passages that directly address his question. Why didn't he include the Philippian jailer's question to Paul and Silas, "Sirs, what must I do to be *saved*?" and their clear response—"*Believe in the Lord Jesus, and you will be saved*" (Acts 16:30–31; italics added)?

Bell's first chapter references Romans 10 (p. 9), but omits the very verse from that Bible chapter which answers Bell's own question. Paul declares in Romans 10:9, "If you *confess* with your mouth, 'Jesus is Lord,' and *believe* in your heart that God raised him from the dead, you will be *saved*" (italics added). Note that Paul says we are saved when we believe and confess, so he would have dismissed Bell's false choice: "Is it what you say, or who you are, or what you do…" (p. 16). Paul would simply declare that when you *are* a new creation in Christ (2 Cor. 5:17), then you will joyfully *say* "Jesus is Lord" and strive to *do* good works which demonstrate the Lord's authority. You wouldn't know it from reading Bell's opening chapter, but Scripture really is that straightforward.

Bell writes an entire chapter on Scripture's supposed confusion on salvation, but omits the Bible's most famous verse on the subject. Jesus says as clearly as possible that "whoever *believes* in [God's only Son] shall not perish but have eternal life" (John 3:16; italics added). And two verses later, Jesus becomes uncomfortably specific about what happens to those who don't believe, declaring that "whoever does *not believe stands condemned* already because he has *not believed* in the name of God's one and only Son" (John 3:18; italics added).

Bell also ignores Peter's promise to the Gentile Cornelius, "All the prophets testify about [Jesus] that everyone who *believes* in him receives forgiveness of sins through his name" (Acts 10:43). And he overlooks Jesus' statement, "The work of God is this: to *believe* in the one he has sent" (John 6:29). Such texts are critically important to address when asking the tough questions about the Bible's views of salvation.

Is Belief Enough?

Bell concludes chapter one with a preemptive counterstrike against those who might raise these salvation passages. He suggests that we aren't saved by believing in Jesus, for even demons believe there is a God and that Jesus is his Son (James 2:19; Matt. 8:28–29). Since demons aren't saved, why should we think that salvation comes by believing in Jesus (p. 18)? The evangelical answer is fairly simple. Both we humans and Scripture use "belief" in two, importantly different senses. In the weak sense, belief means "intellectual assent," such as when I say, "I believe that exercise is good for me." In the strong sense, belief means "hearty trust" or "commitment." I display this belief only when I act on what I know, such as when I get off the couch and go for a jog.

Demons believe in Jesus only in the weak sense. They know that Jesus is God, but they refuse to commit themselves to him. We know this because they are demons, and as such they lack the good works which demonstrate true faith. Thus, the unfaithful "belief" of demons does not disqualify the numerous Scripture passages which claim we are saved by repenting of our sin and believing in Jesus.

Finally, Bell raises a theological problem with the idea of believing in Jesus. He asks how evangelicals can say they are saved by grace if they must do something—namely believe in Jesus—to receive this grace. He writes that if God requires us to believe in Jesus, and since belief is something we must *do*, then we aren't really saved by God's grace, but rather by our own act of faith which merits our forgiveness (p. 11).

Actually, evangelicals hold that faith is an open hand, a passive receiving of God's precious gift to anyone who accepts it. As a child must reach out to receive his Christmas present, but earns no credit for taking it, so we must gratefully accept God's gift of salvation. No child thinks they earned their present because they took it—and no Christian thinks they earned their salvation because they put their faith in Christ.

What about Evil?

I began this chapter with the observation that because we are *finite*, every quest to understand our infinite God will end in unresolved mysteries. We shouldn't run from tension or paradox in our knowledge of God; rather, we should accept our intellectual limitations as a sign that we are in the right neighborhood. If you sense that as you answer your theological question your reach exceeds your grasp, there is a good chance that you are talking about God.

Besides the doctrine of God, a second area that will always end in mystery is any question that is connected to the *fall* (Adam and Eve's disobedience, and fall into sin). How could a person's morally good will—a will created by God—turn bad? Why would an all-powerful and all-loving God even allow it? Why doesn't God step in and stop the suffering caused by human sin? Even more troubling, why doesn't he empty hell and free everyone? We don't know. The fall and its consequences are like a misshaped jigsaw puzzle piece. No matter how hard we twist and cram, we can't fit its angular and grotesque form into our picture of God.

It's not supposed to fit, because it's the fall. The fall is evil, and for that reason it should never make sense. As Cornelius Plantinga Jr. explains in his breviary of sin, the fall and its devastating effects are simply "not the way it's supposed to be." The fall and its consequences are damnable, tragic, and out of sync with what even our human hearts tell us a life of love, joy, and peace should be like. If we could ever wrap our minds around evil and declare, "I get it now! I understand why the fall occurred and why God allows everlasting torment in hell," we would only prove that we are no longer talking about evil. We would be chattering about a weak, domesticated evil, a superficial evil that makes sense only because of our foolish belief that if we can somehow identify it, understand it, and limit it we can then deal with it—apart from God.

Richard Muller once told my seminary class that when it comes to the problem of evil—If God is all-powerful and all-good, why is there evil?—we must choose whether we are going to have a God problem or an evil problem. It's tempting to loosen up one of God's perfections—usually his power—to explain the existence of evil. Many people say that God does not want evil but he risked it when he granted us freedom. There is truth in this—God does not desire evil and we are genuinely free—but the situation is undoubtedly more complex. If we solve the problem of evil by saying the omnipotent God cannot guarantee what his creatures freely choose, then we have saddled ourselves with an even larger God problem. Better to believe that God is all-powerful and all-loving and wrestle with evil than to weaken one aspect of God to make room for evil.

Is Your God Too Small?

Bell's book seems to fall into this trap, for it begins with a rhetorically powerful story that uses the existence of evil in order to construct a one-dimensional view of God. Bell explains that an art show at his church had included a work which used a quote from Mahatma Gandhi. During the show, someone attached a note to the Gandhi piece which said, "Reality check: He's in hell" (p. 1).

Bell responds:

> "Really?
> Gandhi's in hell?
> He is?
> We have confirmation of this?
> Somebody knows this?
> Without a doubt?
> And that somebody decided to take on the responsibility
> of letting the rest of us know?" (pp. 1–2)

Bell further explains that a God who sends people like Gandhi to hell could hardly be considered loving. This is how Bell put it in his promotional video for *Love Wins*:

> Will only a few select people make it to heaven? And will billions and billions of people burn forever in hell? And

if that's the case, how do you become one of the few? Is it what you believe or what you say or what you do or who you know or something that happens in your heart? Or do you need to be initiated or baptized or take a class or converted or being born again? [sic]. How does one become one of these few?

And then there is the question behind the questions. The real question [is]: "What is God like?" Because millions and millions of people were taught that the primary message, the center of the gospel of Jesus, is that God is going to send you to hell unless you believe in Jesus. And so what gets subtly sort of caught and taught is that Jesus rescues you from God. But what kind of God is that, that we would need to be rescued from this God? How could that God ever be good? How could that God ever be trusted? And how could that ever be good news?

This is why lots of people want nothing to do with the Christian faith. They see it as an endless list of absurdities and inconsistencies and they say, "Why would I ever want to be a part of that?" See, what we believe about heaven and hell is incredibly important because it exposes what we believe about who God is and what God is like. What you discover in the Bible is so surprising, unexpected, and beautiful, that whatever we've been told and been taught, the good news is actually better than that, better than we could ever imagine.

The good news is that love wins.(vimeo.com/20272585)

My colleague Jeremy Grinnell thought that a similarly moving argument could be made from the other direction, so he wrote a brief piece to illustrate how that might go. Grinnell is not defending this equally lopsided view of God, but simply trying to show that Bell's story describes only one aspect of the multilayered character of God. Grinnell wrote,

> Several years ago I was touring a holocaust museum, and I was deeply moved by the images of suffering and inhuman brutality that I saw there. Near the end of the tour on the wall was a picture of Hitler standing in front of the Eiffel Tower in Paris. I and many who were with me were struck by the idea of Hitler enjoying the beauties of Paris while at the same moment one of the greatest genocides the world has ever known was being carried out on his orders.
>
> But apparently not everyone saw it exactly the same way, for somebody had attached a handwritten note to the picture, and on the note they had written, "It's okay because God forgave Hitler too."
>
> God forgave Hitler? He did? And someone knows this for sure? And felt the need for the rest of us to know? Do the most evil and unrepentant people in history, remaining what they are, still make it to heaven?
>
> And then there's the question behind the question. The real question is, "What is God like?" Because millions and millions were taught that the primary message of the gospel of Jesus Christ is that God is willing to forgive everybody no matter who they are or what evils they've committed against the rest of us. So what gets subtly sort of caught and taught is that God is willing to forgive the perpetrators of evil, regardless of whether or not their victims ever see justice. That God is willing to let all things slide. Everything. But what kind of God is that? Can a God so uninterested in

justice be good? How can that God ever be trusted? How could that ever be good news?

This is why lots of people want nothing to do with the Christian faith. They see it as an endless list of absurdities and inconsistencies, and say, "Why would I ever want to be a part of that?"

See, what we believe about heaven and hell is incredibly important because it exposes what we believe about who God is and what God is like. What you discover in the Bible is so surprising, and unexpected, and beautiful, that whatever we've been told or taught, the good news is even better than that, better than we can ever imagine. It means pure and perfect justice, no wrong accusations, no punishments that don't fit the crime, no hidden motives, no unaccounted pains or sorrows, but overflowing compensation for anyone who's ever been hurt or betrayed.

The good news is that God's "justice wins."

The takeaway from these dueling stories is that in order to even begin to understand God we need full and equal parts of divine love *and* divine justice. God is love (1 John 4:8) and God is holy (1 Peter 1:16). He is neither more loving than he is holy, nor more holy than loving. God's love is holy, and his holiness is love. He is holy love and loving holiness.

Love and holiness are not competing perfections, but opposite ends of a continuum (as perceived by our finite minds) that reinforce one other. Each perfection needs the other to be what it is. Love without holiness becomes a squishy sentimentality, and holiness without love becomes an unholy focus on keeping the rules. Holiness isn't holy if it's not loving, and love isn't love if it's not holy. Chapter nine will explain how, despite Bell's emphasis on God's love, his diminished view of God's holiness sells short God's love, leaving us with a God who is neither entirely holy nor entirely loving.

Bell would have done better to follow the example of the apostle Paul, who raised the question of hell in Romans 9–11. Paul pondered how a loving and just God could save Jacob but not Esau, and after wrestling with the issue he concluded that he could only bow before the mystery of God. God is both loving and just, though he could not explain how. Paul simply worshiped: "Oh, the depth of the riches of the wisdom and knowledge of God! How unsearchable his judgments, and his paths beyond tracing out!" (Rom. 11:33).

Conclusion

I will suggest throughout this book that Bell's one-dimensional God lacks the greater, more mysterious transcendence of the Christian God. Bell's view of God too often reads like a souped-up version of us—a God made more in our image than we in his. Is Bell really talking about the biblical God, or just about ourselves in a really loud voice?

Bell concludes his opening chapter by noting that even though we start our pursuit of God with mystery, it isn't enough to stay there: "But this isn't a book of questions. It's a book of responses to these questions." I couldn't agree more. It's not enough to wallow in our questions; we need answers. And so, with Bell, we turn to God's revelation.

Revelation 2

magine that you're in the market for a used car. You can't afford much, because your job is tenuous, but you need something reliable to commute to work daily. You head to Bob's All-Star Pre-Owned Cars because you went to school with his son, Ken, who now works for his father. You need a deal.

The struggling economy has significantly depleted Bob's stock of "all-star" cars, but Ken shows you an older sedan that's just outside your price range. The car looks (and smells) great, but you remember a consumer alert that mentioned transmission problems with that year's make and model. You share your fears with Ken, who responds with a great deal—just what you were hoping to land.

"Listen," he begins, "I know the price may be a bit of a stretch, and it may not be the most comfortable deal for you. But if you really want this car, I'll put your mind at ease by throwing in a six-month, money-back guarantee. If you aren't completely satisfied with this car for any reason—say the transmission goes or you simply tire of the color—we'll take it back and refund whatever you paid. Worst-case scenario, you drove a car on us for six months."

You still worry that the cost is more than you can afford, but with such a generous guarantee, how could you go wrong? You sign the papers and drive your sweet ride home. Three months later, when you hear thumping in the transmission, you cruise back to All-Star Cars, only to learn that Ken joined the Peace Corps. No matter. You show your papers to Bob. But Bob looks bewildered.

"Ken wasn't authorized to make this warranty," he shrugged. "That was a temporary program we ran ten years ago to support our troops. It was only good for veterans and their families, and it expired six months later. See here in the fine print?" Ouch!

Consider another hypothetical story. Like a lot of North Americans, you're struggling with obesity. You confide in your physician friend, Sam, that you think you should try to lose at least one of your chins. He replies that, as a doctor, he would tell you that dieting is always a good idea. However, as your friend who knows how much you enjoy cheeseburgers smothered in mayonnaise, he assures you that if you don't want to settle for rice cakes and celery sticks, you could wait five years and then trim down with gastric bypass surgery or one of the weight loss drugs that pharmaceutical companies are beginning to churn out.

You take Sam's advice, glad for a doctor who appreciates the big picture. But three years later your deep-fried lifestyle has moved you from overweight to morbidly obese. Now even your chins have chins, so you make an appointment to see about that surgery. Dr. Sam runs some tests, then sighs and says you are not a candidate for gastric bypass surgery because your swollen heart couldn't endure the procedure. Worse yet, you have contracted type 2 diabetes, so your final few years are not going to be much fun.

Check the Fine Print

Both Ken and Sam made promises that sounded great at the point of sale. However, neither of their promises turned out to be true, and neither of them was authorized to promise what he did. This is precisely the problem that many evangelicals have with Rob Bell's promises—some stated and some implied—in *Love Wins.* It's not true, as some say, that we evangelicals are stingy people who take delight in self-righteously consigning others to hell.

We weep for anyone who goes to hell, and that is why we are questioning the apparent claims in *Love Wins.* As Ken's promise encouraged you to buy a lemon and Dr. Sam's reassurance contributed to your swift and painful death, so Bell's wishful words may unwittingly lead more people to hell. Bell makes the same kind of guarantee as Ken and Sam, promising readers that they will have a future opportunity to fix whatever mistakes they have made in this life. He assures them that they will have numerous chances to be "saved" after they die. They will even be able to leave hell if they want.

In what seems to be Bell's own view—or at least what most readers will understandably take as his view—he says that

> there are others who ask, if you get another chance after you die, why limit that chance to a one-off immediately after death? And so they expand the possibilities, trusting that there will be endless opportunities in an endless amount of time for people to say yes to God.

As long as it takes, in other words. (pp. 106–7)

It's easy for readers to become so excited over the promise of postmortem salvation (a second chance after death) that they might not ask some basic questions:

Is it true?

How does Bell know that it's true?

Who has authorized him to make such a guarantee?

For evangelicals, it isn't enough for Bell to say on his own authority that a loving God would always give condemned sinners as many chances as they need, even after death, to accept the gift of salvation. In fact, why would God *have* to do this? What requires God to act in ways that we would desire him to act? If this unending, even-after-death offer of salvation is what a loving God *must* do, then why hasn't he told us this explicitly through the many prophets, gospel writers, and epistle authors inspired by the Holy Spirit? Why would a God who "loves" enough to empty hell want to frighten people now with numerous warnings that sound like hell lasts forever? If God is merely using such hellish language to scare us into living for him, aren't we stuck with a cynical view of God? God is loving, even more than Bell says. But God is also holy and just, which complicates our ability to say what his love must do.

Godly Hopes and Human Wishes

Neither will it do for Bell to suggest that "Christian hope" requires multiple chances for salvation after death. He seemed shocked by a Christian who said there was no hope for a deceased atheist. "No hope?" he asked. "Is that the Christian message? 'No hope'? Is that what Jesus offers the world? Is this the sacred calling of Christians—to announce that there's no hope?" (pp. 3–4).

I appreciate Bell's desire to offer hope. It is excruciatingly difficult to tell a student, "Sorry, you're going to fail this program," or a patient, "Sorry, but it looks like you're going to die." No one wants to deliver horrible, hopeless news, so we understandably flail and grasp for any reason that may offer a path to recovery. We can offer a student additional tutoring or an extra-credit assignment; we can suggest a patient try one more experimental drug or procedure. But there comes a time when the kindest thing that we can tell someone is, "Listen, I'm not going to offer more than I can deliver. I'm not going to overpromise. The truth is that I am out of options. And you might be, too. You are going to fail; you are going to die."

Our hopes are only as strong as the reasons we have for holding them. Some hopes are nothing more than a wish—I hope that it doesn't rain tomorrow or that my team will win the game. But Christian hope, the kind that makes the top cut with faith and love (1 Cor. 13:13), is grounded in the promises of God. Such hope is "an anchor for the soul, firm and secure" (Heb. 6:19), because it rests in what "God, who does not lie, promised before the beginning of time" (Titus 1:2).

I *wish* that God would empty hell, that he would save everyone who has ever lived. But I can't say I *hope* for that, because I don't have a promise from God to hang my hope on. Christians may have lots of good wishes for deceased atheists, but we don't have hope. Not because we are mean or stingy, but because we dare not offer more hope than God promises in Scripture. That would be false hope, the cruelest hope of all.

What the Bible Says

The essential issue, then, is not what we want to be true but what the Bible says. The apostle Paul explains, "For everything that was written in the past was written to teach us, so that through the endurance taught in the Scriptures and the encouragement they provide we might have hope" (Rom. 15:4). No one is authorized to promise anything from God that is not revealed in Scripture. So we must ask, does Bell have a Word from God which promises that sinners will have multiple chances to leave hell, and does he adequately address the biblical texts which seem to imply the contrary?

The short answer is no. Bell does not cite one biblical passage which says that sinners can change their minds (and hearts) and leave hell if they so desire. His biblical basis for postmortem salvation seems to be the passages in Scripture which speak of God's "cosmic" salvation—that is, God's promise to restore the entire world. Bell writes approvingly of the "long tradition of Christians who believe that God will ultimately restore everything and everybody, because Jesus says in Matthew 19 that there will be a 'renewal of all things,' Peter says in Acts 3 that Jesus will 'restore everything,' and Paul says in Colossians 1 that through Christ 'God was pleased to…reconcile to himself all things, whether things on earth or things in heaven'" (p. 107). Since Scripture teaches that "all things" will be renewed or reconciled to Christ, and since it's obvious that many people die without knowledge or acceptance of God, Bell concludes that these people will have new opportunities to be saved in the afterlife.

Bell's logic is sound, but what about his premise that Scripture teaches that every person will be saved as part of the renewal of "all things"? These texts can't bear the weight that advocates of post-mortem salvation place on them. Scripture often speaks of a marvelous, cosmic salvation (more on this in chapter 3), but the restoration of all things does not necessarily mean that every last plant, animal, or person that ever lived will return to the New Earth. Terms such as "all" and "world" can be used to denote every member of a class, as in "God saw all that he had made, and it was very good" (Genesis 1:31). But these terms can also be used more generally, as when "the whole town went out to meet Jesus" (Matthew 8:34). Not every person in the world went after Jesus, but enough did that the Pharisees could complain that "the whole world has gone after him" (John 12:19). Moreover, Scripture is clear that some things-including some people-will not inherit the kingdom of God. Satan and his fallen angels will suffer forever in hell, for instance, so there are some (higher than human) people whom God will not save. If angelic persons are not offered a second chance to escape, then what logic requires that all human persons must?

Troublesome Texts

So Bell offers no biblical passage which promises postmortem salvation, and his argument from what universalistic texts supposedly imply isn't persuasive either. Worse, there are biblical texts which indicate that the suffering in hell lasts forever. When I first learned of Bell's book, I immediately wondered how he would interpret the lake of fire mentioned near the end of Scripture and Jesus' story of the rich man and Lazarus. Both of these biblical texts strongly suggest that sinners in hell are not offered a second chance. What would Bell make of them?

Bell did not include the lake of fire in his chapter on hell—a chapter which implies that it includes every biblical passage which addresses everlasting, fiery torment. Bell begins the "hell" chapter by promising, "I want to show you every single verse in the Bible in which we find the actual word 'hell'" (p. 64), and then after discussing *sheol* in the Old Testament and Jesus' twelve mentions of *gehenna*, he concludes, "And that's it. Those are all of the mentions of 'hell' in the Bible" (p. 69). After two more paragraphs on the terms *Tartarus* and *Hades*, he similarly concludes, "Anything you have ever heard people say about the actual word 'hell' in the Bible they got from those verses you just read" (p. 69).

That statement is technically true but factually misleading. It's true that Bell covered every instance of the Greek term *gehenna*, but not everything evangelicals say about hell comes "from those verses you just read." Much of what we know about hell comes from verses he didn't mention. Consider Revelation 20:10–15, which warns of a lake of fire:

> And the devil, who deceived them, was thrown into the lake of burning sulfur, where the beast and the false prophet had been thrown. They will be tormented day and night for ever and ever…Then death and Hades were thrown into the lake of fire. The lake of fire is the second death. Anyone whose name was not found written in the book of life was thrown into the lake of fire.

Love Wins does not include these verses in its examination of hell. Their description of final and everlasting judgment comes so close to the end of the biblical story that it is hard to say how they leave room for postmortem salvation.

Bell appears to try in a later chapter, for he mentions a lake of fire that appears in "the Book of Revelation, a complex, enigmatic letter…filled with scenes of scrolls and robes and angels and plagues and trumpets and horses and dragons and beasts and bowls and prostitutes and horses." He implies that this letter is written in such "an apocalyptic, heavily symbolic way" that we can't say what much of it means (pp. 111–12). Yet three pages later Bell says that the symbolism of heaven's gates never shutting (Rev. 21:25) means that "people are free to come and go," implying that God keeps the door open for postmortem, universal salvation (pp. 114–15). But isn't this a more difficult symbol to interpret than the lake of fire? How does Bell conclude that an open gate signifies salvation but that a lake of burning sulfur may not be hell? In literary history, a lake of burning sulfur has consistently symbolized hell.

Bell gives more attention to Jesus' story of the rich man and Lazarus. In this ultimate reversal of fortune, poor Lazarus dies and is carried by angels to Abraham's side, while the rich man who scornfully ignored Lazarus's plight ends up in Hades. This is a difficult passage for postmortem salvation, for Jesus does not hint that the rich man has an opportunity to leave his unending torment. On the contrary, Jesus has Abraham make the point to the rich man that "between us and you a great chasm has been set in place, so that those who want to go from here to you cannot, nor can anyone cross over from there to us" (Luke 16:26). All that remains is for the rich man to beg Abraham to send Lazarus to warn his brothers to repent and avoid coming to the place of no return.

Centuries of Christians have read Jesus' story in this straightforward way. But Bell offers a hidden reason why the rich man is unable to leave his suffering in hell, and it lies in the rich man's request to "send Lazarus." Not only does the rich man ask Abraham to "send Lazarus" to warn his brothers, but he begs Abraham to "send Lazarus to dip the tip of his finger in water and cool my tongue, because I am in agony in this fire" (Luke 26:24). Bell observes,

> When you get someone water, you're serving them.
>
> The rich man wants Lazarus to serve him.
>
> In their previous life, the rich man saw himself as better than Lazarus, and now, in hell, the rich man *still* sees himself as above Lazarus. It's no wonder Abraham says there's a chasm that can't be crossed. The chasm is the rich man's heart! It hasn't changed, even in death and torment and agony. He's still clinging to the old hierarchy. He still thinks he's better. (p. 75; italics original)

And so Bell suggests that this story offers a ray of hope; if the rich man would just humble himself, he would be able to escape his torment.

Bell would have a stronger argument if the rich man had asked Lazarus to bring him an apple martini with a splash of lime. The rich man didn't ask for a drink that a servant might bring to his lord; he didn't even ask for so much as a drink! He didn't beg for a tall glass of anything, but just a drop of water that he could suck from Lazarus's finger. Does that really sound like someone who thought he was "above Lazarus," or is it more plausible to believe that hell had so humbled the rich man that he didn't care that the scorned Lazarus saw his dreadful despair, as long as Lazarus's visit might bring momentary relief from his agony?

Further proof that the rich man was not "still clinging to the old hierarchy" is his concern for his brothers. The rich man seems to have genuinely changed, for rather than self-ishly damn everyone else once he realized his fate was sealed, he compassionately wanted his family to be saved—and he asked that the bearer of that salvation be Lazarus, the very person his family had despised.

I wish Bell had told us where he learned his interpretation of this story. Who else in church history has thought that this is the point of Jesus' story? Bell doesn't say, so I can only evaluate his interpretation by the argument he gave. I see no reason to think that he is right, and many ways that his interpretation is clearly wrong.

What Preachers Say

I appreciate that Bell is willing to risk his reputation as an evangelical pastor in order to promote an endlessly positive message of multiple chances for salvation after we die. I think he genuinely believes this, and wants everyone else to believe and bask in it too. But wanting something to be true does not make it true.

Salesman Ken believed he was doing you a favor as a friend, offering a way out if you didn't like the car you were stretching to buy. Dr. Sam believed you had plenty of options to fix later what your bad diet was ruining today. It turned out both were wrong, in ways that were pretty hard to swallow. But neither losing a car nor losing your life is as devastating as learning, too late, that you do not have the way out of hell you were promised. If you were angry with Ken and Sam when you realized they were wrong, imagine how you would feel if you discovered that the Bible doesn't promise what Bell says it does.

It's important to add that Bell wants everyone to repent and follow Jesus now. He does not want anyone to go to hell, not even for a minute. But once he promises a second chance after we die, he is unable to say why it is imperative that we convert now. He can only suggest, "While we may get other opportunities, we won't get the one right in front of us again. That specific moment will pass and we will not see it again. It comes, it's here, it goes, and then it's gone" (p. 197).

This is a game effort, but a thinking person might just shrug their shoulders and say, so what? What is so crucially important about this one moment that I must repent of my selfishness and live for Jesus now? I have an eternity of unending moments ahead of me, so why shouldn't I milk this life by doing whatever I want and then give my heart to Jesus when the next life begins? If I have forever to correct whatever sins I've committed in this life, how exactly is it "vitally important [that] we take our choices here and now as seriously as we possibly can because they matter more than we can begin to imagine" (p. 197)?

Bell apparently wants to have it both ways: our choices are vitally important now, but we can cancel them out whenever we want in the next life. He does not explain how both can be true, but simply asserts that they are. He may not want people to use his book as an excuse not to follow Jesus now, but it is easy to see how many could logically draw this conclusion.

Conclusion

We can readily avoid this danger by following a simple rule: speak when the Bible speaks and remain quiet when the Bible is silent. The Bible never promises postmortem salvation, but it repeatedly warns about unending torment in hell. Ministers of the Word should conform to God's revelation, proclaiming its clear warnings and refusing to speculate where Scripture does not. If God wanted people to know they would have a second chance after death, he would have told them. Since he didn't—and since his repeated warnings about hell run hard in the other direction—those who assert there is a chance for postmortem salvation inadvertently claim to know better than God what God should have included in his Word.

Rather than speculate where Scripture is silent, we should proclaim God's glorious hope for the world, namely, that "God so loved the world that he gave his one and only Son, that whoever believes in him shall not perish but have eternal life" (John 3:16). There is no need to reach higher and offer promises that God didn't make and we can't deliver. Doing so turns biblical hope into false hope, the cruelest hope of all.

Heaven

3

Rob Bell's description of heaven—"Here Is the New There"—is my favorite section in *Love Wins*. He and I grew up in similar, theologically conservative churches which taught us to love Jesus and the Bible. We both thank God for this evangelical heritage. In his last chapter, Bell writes of the prayer he said as a child in which he knelt beside his bed and invited Jesus into his heart: "It meant something significant then and it continues to have profound significance for me. That prayer was a defining moment in my life" (p. 194). We wouldn't trade our pietistic upbringing for anything, but we agree that our evangelical heritage suffered from an overly Platonic (otherworldly) view of heaven. This chapter will affirm Bell's recovery of the earthiness of our end, even as it challenges several of his innovative suggestions about heaven.

Platonic Heavens vs. the New Earth

Plato is arguably the greatest Western philosopher of all time (428/427–348/347 BCE), but he unfortunately divided the world into two separate parts. He said that the upper story, what he called the Forms, is the real world of eternal, unchanging ideals. The lower story, where we live, is the world of Matter. This material world isn't real, but merely consists of physical copies of those Forms which exist in that higher, spiritual world.

> Down here we have cows. Up there is the perfect ideal of "cowness."
> Down here we have trees. Up there exists the unchanging principle of "treeness."
> Down here we have the University of Michigan football team. Up there we have the eternal form of "mediocrity" (unlike Bell, I was raised in Ohio).

Plato taught that we humans are essentially souls who used to live in that higher, immaterial world of the Forms. But now our souls are trapped in this lower, material world, chained by the prison of our bodies. According to the Platonic view, rather than succumb to our pressing material needs and pleasures, we must remember that this physical world isn't real. We should meditate on the higher, spiritual reality, because someday we will shed our bodies, leave this inferior, earthy realm, and go to heaven, where our souls will twinkle and shine forever.

This Platonic dualism—heaven is good, the earth is bad; my soul is good, my body is bad—was passed along to the Neoplatonists (third century CE), a group which included such thinkers as Plotinus, Porphyry, and one of the most amusing names in the history of philosophy, Ammonius Saccas (also the name of my fantasy football team). These Neoplatonists influenced Augustine of Hippo, who in the fourth century converted to their philosophy on his way to becoming a Christian.

Augustine knew that the Platonists wrongly believed that the physical world was evil, but he thought they rightly held that the material world was inferior to that higher, spiritual reality. Since Augustine is the most important theologian in church history, he led centuries of Christians to think that the higher world of heaven is the only real world and this earthly life doesn't count for much.

Even today, many best-selling books—evangelical books included—argue something like this: "Life on earth is just the dress rehearsal before the real production...Earth is the staging area, the preschool, the tryout for your life in eternity. It is the practice workout before the actual game, the warm-up lap before the race begins" (Warren, p. 36). Favorite evangelical songs rejoice, "This world is not my home, I'm just a passin' through," and someday, the songs say, the believer will leave this world: "I'll fly away...Like a bird from prison bars has flown, I'll fly away." It's difficult to sit through many sermons or Christian songs without being reminded that this world isn't real and that the spiritual realm of heaven is our permanent, eternal home.

Many Christians are now challenging this Platonic view of heaven (see, for example, my *Heaven Is a Place on Earth*; N. T. Wright, *Surprised by Hope*; Nathan Bierma, *Bringing Heaven Down to Earth*; or Randy Alcorn, *Heaven*). We realize that the Bible never speaks of heaven as the endgame, but repeatedly says that Jesus will return to restore this creation and live with his people on the new earth (Isa. 65:17; 2 Peter 3:13; Rev. 21:1). Unlike the leaders of many other religions, who declare that the good stuff happens high up and far away, Jesus says that the kingdom of God comes to earth (or, more precisely, that it has come, is coming, and will fully come).

This "earthy" focus seems to be a Christian distinctive, for the followers of other religions generally long to go someplace better, holier, or more spiritual than mere earth. Muslims want to go to paradise, Buddhists yearn to enter nirvana, and some Native Americans dream of the "Happy Hunting Grounds" in the sky. Jesus is the only major religious leader who instructs followers not to pray to be taken away but to pray for the kingdom to come "on earth as it is in heaven" (Matt. 6:10). This is why Scripture concludes with John's Hallelujah Chorus. When Jesus returns, the seventh angel will sound his trumpet and shout, "The kingdom of the world has become the kingdom of our Lord and of his Messiah, and he will reign for ever and ever" (Rev. 11:15).

So Bell rightly challenges the common, Platonic view that Christians will spend forever floating in the celestial clouds, wearing white robes and strumming harps. As he says, the Jewish prophets "did not talk about a future life *somewhere else*, because they anticipated a coming day when the world would be restored, renewed, and redeemed and there would be peace on earth" (p. 40; italics original). I could not agree more. Many Christians, evangelicals included, need to hear this deeply biblical message.

A Cautionary Recovery of Heaven

I have only a few issues with Bell's welcome recovery of the earthiness of our salvation—related both to how he communicates and to what he is trying to communicate. First, I wish he had used the biblical term "new earth" rather than "heaven." As N. T. Wright said in *Surprised by Hope: Rethinking Heaven, the Resurrection, and the Mission of the Church* about

Randy Alcorn's book, *Heaven*, Bell has the right content but the wrong word (Wright, p. 298). As long as we use the term "heaven" for our biblical hope, many Christians will continue to think of the end in Platonic categories. Rather than use the term "heaven" for our earthly redemption, we should clarify the difference between the Platonic and Christian view by consistently using the biblical language of "new heaven and new earth" (noting that "heaven" in this phrase means the sky rather than some spiritual realm which transcends creation).

Second, Bell seems to succumb to Plato's influence when he says the Greek term *aion* "is often translated as 'eternal' in English, which is an altogether different word from 'forever.'" He explains that "forever, as a uniform measurement of time, like days and years, marching endlessly into the future...[is] not a category or concept we find in the Bible. This is why a lot of translators choose to translate *aion* as 'eternal.' By this they don't mean the literal passing of time; they mean transcending time, belonging to another realm altogether" (p. 58; italics original).

Actually, the adjectival form of *aion* is the way the Greeks expressed our concept of "forever." Jesus said that those who believe in him will have *zoen aionion*—a life that never ends (John 3:16). Jesus is not telling us that we will transcend time or be taken up into some higher, supernatural realm, for as bodily creatures we will always live within the boundaries of space and time. We will never step outside of time into God's realm, but we will live forever in our redeemed creation. Scripture describes this as everlasting life, a life that begins in this age (*aion*) and continues through every age to come. Thus, the biblical writers do understand "forever" as "a uniform measurement of time, like days and years, marching endlessly into the future," and they describe this passing of time with the adjectival form of the term *aion*.

Third, while I appreciate Bell's question about why there would be tears in heaven, I don't think this suggests a postmortem or universal salvation. Bell rightly wonders how missing loved ones wouldn't spoil the pleasure of heaven. If they aren't with us then they must be in hell. How could we know that and still rejoice in our salvation (p. 25)? This is one of those excruciatingly hard questions that we must chalk up to the fall. I said in chapter one that everything connected to the fall is going to end in deep mystery, and this is one of those things. I can't understand how I will enjoy the new earth if someone I love isn't there, but I believe my tears for them will somehow be wiped away (Rev. 21:4). Our hearts ache to know something more, but we have to respect the impenetrable mystery of the fall. Better to leave some questions unresolved than attempt to tame the wild fury of evil.

What Is New on the New Earth?

Bell rightly says that Scripture teaches us to long for the new earth, but while he powerfully emphasizes the "earth" part of this phrase, he gives too little attention to what is "new." Bell is so focused on pointing out that our final destiny will be here that he neglects the many ways it will be different. Throughout this chapter I found myself asking, "But what is *new* about the new earth?" The new earth is the earth, so it will be similar to what we have now, but it will also be new, so something will be different. What is this dissimilarity? Bell doesn't seem to think there will be much difference, and so his view of the present turns out to be too much like the future, and his view of the future becomes too much like the present.

1. Bell's present is too much like the future.

Bell seems to have what theologians call a "realized eschatology," for he declares that the *eschaton* (the end) is already here. He uses his redefinition of *aion* to conclude that heaven is an intensity of experience that may be enjoyed in each moment of our present lives. He writes that "when Jesus talked about heaven, he was talking about our present *eternal, intense, real* experiences of joy, peace, and love in this life, this side of death *and* the age to come. Heaven for Jesus wasn't just 'someday'; it was a present reality. Jesus blurs the lines, inviting the rich man, and us, into the merging of heaven and earth, the future and present, *here* and *now*" (pp. 58–59; italics original). Bell adds that

> Jesus invites us,
> in this life,
> in this broken, beautiful world,
> to experience the life of heaven now. (p. 62)

Bell rightly contends that "eternal life doesn't start when we die; it starts now" (p. 59), but he wrongly "blurs the line" between the happiness of our present life and the unimaginable joy of living in the presence of Jesus on the new earth. The kingdom has already come, but it also is not yet. We pray for the kingdom to come in its fullness, but only Jesus can finally bring it. We should live in loving and peaceful ways that anticipate the glories of Christ's kingdom, but at the end of the day we must wait for it.

Bell's message that heaven is already here sounds thrilling—we can have heaven on earth now!—but ultimately it fails to satisfy. If the fullness of heaven is already on earth—if there is not much difference between our present and our future—then we don't have much to look forward to. This life, with its exhilarating but ultimately unfulfilling joys, is as good as it gets.

2. Bell's future will be too much like the present.

Christians with a Platonic view of the world (heaven is good and the earth is bad) often create a vast chasm between our present life and the next. Our present, earthly life is full of struggle and growth, so our future, heavenly life must be perfect in every way. One esteemed theologian wrote that "we will not grow in heaven," for there "we will have perfect knowledge" that will achieve "a state of completion beyond which there can be no advance" (Erickson, p. 410).

Bell rightly rejects this Platonized ideal of static perfection in heaven. He correctly observes, "Much of the speculation about heaven—and, more important, the confusion—comes from the idea that in the blink of an eye we will automatically become totally different people who 'know' everything" (p. 51). I concur that we will never bottom out and become bored in the next life, for we will forever continue to grow in our knowledge of God, ourselves, and this world. We were placed here by God to govern this world on his behalf, and we will continue to do that, only better, on the new earth. As Bell aptly declares, "We were made to explore and discover and learn and create and shape and form and engage this world" (p. 48), and we will do that forever, on the new earth and in the presence of Jesus.

So I appreciate Bell's point that we will continue to grow and mature in heaven. However, I wish he had distinguished between different kinds of growth. Bell assumes that we will continue to grow not only in our knowledge of God and the world, but also in our moral actions. Note how in the quotation above he seamlessly shifts from *epistemological* (knowledge) to *ethical* (moral) categories, from "the idea that in the blink of an eye we will automatically become totally different people who 'know' everything" to the idea that "our heart, our character, our desires, our longings," too, will be changed—though more slowly.

Heart, character, desires, and *longings* refer to moral qualities. I understand why we will grow in knowledge in heaven, but why does Bell suggest we will grow morally? Does he think there will be sin in heaven? Will the God who prohibited anyone but Moses from touching Mount Sinai and anyone but the high priest from entering the Holy of Holies allow the whole bunch of unreformed sinners into his presence in heaven?

Bell apparently means to say this, for he also declares that "Jesus makes no promise that in the blink of an eye we will suddenly become totally different people who have vastly different tastes, attitudes, and perspectives" (p. 50). Perhaps Jesus didn't make this promise, but John did. He wrote, "We know that when Christ appears, we shall be like him, for we shall see him as he is" (1 John 3:2). Paul agreed, saying that when Jesus appears "we will all be changed—in a flash, in the twinkling of an eye, at the last trumpet." This instantaneous change will be both physical and moral, for we will receive our immortal, resurrection bodies and enjoy Christ's final victory over all sin and death (1 Cor. 15:51–57).

Bell doesn't address these Scripture passages, but instead insists that heaven will be a kind of purgatory. He suggests that we must develop now our "capacity for joy in the world to come" (p. 44), and if we die unprepared we must be purified by the "flames in heaven" until "we can actually handle heaven," with its "bliss, peace, and endless joy" (p. 50).

What about Purgatory?

Protestants don't typically believe in purgatory, partly because it lacks biblical support. Roman Catholics cite 2 Maccabees 12:39–46, which instructs saints to pray that the dead might be delivered from their sins. But this passage appears in the Apocrypha, and so it carries little biblical weight with Protestants. Bell attempts to read purgatory into 1 Corinthians 3:10–15, which says that the day of the Lord will bring a fire that will burn away whatever shoddy work is done in his name (p. 49). But Paul is speaking here about a day of testing for rewards, not an extended period when sinners are purified in heaven.

Protestants also generally agree that the doctrine of purgatory—a time of waiting when deceased humans are sufficiently cleansed to enter heaven—seems to lack sufficient grace. If we must be purified through the arduous process of purgatory, it is hard to avoid the implication that, at least in part, we are doing something to merit our salvation. Does God save us entirely by his grace, or do we still have to earn it through moral improvement, even after death?

This is a larger problem for Bell than for Roman Catholics, for whereas the latter believe that Jesus will empty purgatory when he returns, Bell says that no one is transformed "in the blink of an eye." He apparently holds that the process of learning to love God will go on for a long, indefinite period of time. Everyone must win their way out of purgatory.

Whither Grace in *Love Wins*?

I'll examine this further in subsequent chapters, but it's appropriate to ask now whether *Love Wins* teaches enough saving grace to be Christian. Bell seems to believe that every person is born into the family of God the moment they are conceived, and that they remain in good standing with God as long as they make the right, loving choices. He doesn't appreciate the depths of human depravity—that we all are sinners who have rebelled against a holy God—and so he underestimates the grace that is required to save us. He doesn't seem to think we humans are too awfully bad—at least not bad enough to deserve hell—and so if we truly desire to do so we can purify our souls and save ourselves.

Bell implies that our main problem is not sin—disobedience against God—but mere ignorance. He realizes that we don't often live as we should, but he suggests that this is so because we lack the fuller knowledge that we will gain when we go to heaven:

> It's as if we're currently trying to play the piano while wearing oven mitts.
>
> We can make a noise, sometimes even hit the notes well enough to bang out a melody, but it doesn't sound like it could, or should.
>
> The elements are all there—fingers, keys, strings, ears—but there's something in the way, something inhibiting our ability to fully experience all the possibilities. The apostle Paul writes that now we see "as in a mirror; then we shall see face to face." (p. 61)

For Bell, then, the problem that is "in the way…inhibiting our ability to fully experience all the possibilities" is a form of ignorance. We won't enjoy all that God has for us until we see Jesus "face to face." Most Christians follow John's lead and say that seeing Jesus directly will change us morally, for then "we shall be like him, for we shall see him as he is" (1 John 3:2).

Bell's belief in some type of after-death, purgatorial period prevents him from taking this view, and the only option left is to believe that seeing Jesus directly will inspire us to try harder to please him. But this is consistent with salvation by works, not with the message of grace taught in the Christian gospel.

Bell also implies salvation by works in his illustration of the single mom whose heroic efforts to care for her children while juggling multiple jobs earn her first place in the kingdom. He rightly says that this woman has proved to be faithful with the little that God has given her, but then he suggests that this means she belongs to the kingdom. "She can be trusted," Bell writes.

Is she the last who Jesus says will be first?

Does God say to her, "You're the kind of person I can run the world with"? (p. 53)

Well, I don't know. Is she a Christian? Doesn't it matter whether or not she knows Jesus? Does every good person who admirably endures a difficult life become first in the kingdom, or must people repent of their sin and believe in Jesus even to make it in the door? Bell clearly rejects the latter and, as we will see in future chapters, seems very comfortable with the former. He rightly assumes that none of us stand in God's place. We don't have the ability to look into people's hearts and say who is in or who is out. Nor would we want to. But as we mentioned in chapter one, God has told us what we need to do to be saved, and we should start there when we discourse about life in the kingdom.

Conclusion

There is much to like about Bell's chapter on heaven—especially his emphasis on the non-Platonic earthiness of the afterlife. Bell rightly rejects the squishy sentimentality that supposes the Christian goal is to go to some heavenly otherworld, thoroughly disconnected from God's own good creation. Christianity is an earthy faith: it begins in a sensuous garden, turns on the embodiment of our God, is celebrated with the physical signs of baptism and the Eucharist, and culminates in the physical and spiritual joys of the new earth.

But Bell also proposes a purgatorial view of the afterlife. He depicts life on the new earth as a kind of gradual change in which human beings, having been enlightened by seeing Jesus face-to-face, are further able to reach their moral potential. It's not clear in the book how this portrayal of heaven squares with salvation as a complete and effective act of God. In any case, Bell more fully develops his notions of salvation and the afterlife in his subsequent chapter on hell. That chapter leads into the heart of the controversy over *Love Wins*, and I will examine it next.

Hell

4

The most famous sermon ever preached in America is Jonathan Edwards's 1741 revival message, "Sinners in the Hands of an Angry God." Edwards read his sermon by candlelight, warning the congregation that they deserved to go to hell and urging them to repent before it was too late. Many wept and cried out to God as Edwards's quiet voice reached a climax:

> O Sinner! Consider the fearful danger you are in: 'tis a great furnace of wrath, a wide and bottomless pit, full of the fire of wrath, that you are held over in the hand of that God, whose wrath is provoked and incensed as much against you as against many of the damned in hell; you hang by a slender thread, with the flames of divine wrath flashing about it, and ready every moment to singe it, and burn it asunder; and you have no interest in any Mediator, and nothing to lay hold of to save yourself, nothing to keep off the flames of wrath, nothing of your own, nothing that you

ever have done, nothing that you can do, to induce God to
spare you one moment.(Edwards, p. 98)

Fast-forward to today, when some of the most-discussed
sermons in America are delivered by a pastor who asserts
that Edwards's view of hell is a "misguided and toxic" story
that promotes a "devastating" and "psychologically crushing" understanding of God (pp. viii, 174). "Does God punish
people for thousands of years with infinite, eternal torment
for things they did in their few finite years of life?" Rob Bell
asks rhetorically. "Can God do this, or even allow this, and
still claim to be a loving God?" (p. 2).

How did America move from Edwards to Bell? What
has happened in our culture that makes even conservative
Christians more sympathetic to Bell's "loving" portrayal than
to Edwards's passionate pleas about the dangers of hell? What
has occurred is modernity.

Modern Misgivings

The modern age began in the seventeenth century with the
Enlightenment and rise of modern science, peaked in the
nineteenth and twentieth centuries, and is still chugging along
today (even with the rise of postmodernism). In two words,
modernity values human *reason* and human *autonomy*—the
right of every person and society to judge for themselves
what is right and wrong, good and bad. While this freedom
to judge rationally for ourselves may liberate us from some of
the superstitions of the past, it is devastating when wantonly
applied to Scripture. When autonomous people stand over
God's revelation, they judge for themselves which parts they

will and will not accept. God and his revelation must conform to their own standards and expectations.

The autonomy of the modern world gave rise to theological liberalism, a once-powerful movement which held that every claim of Scripture must be evaluated by the rational, scientific, and "objective" standards of the modern worldview. Please note that I am referring here only to *theological* liberalism. Nothing I say in this chapter should be construed as a critique of other, distinct forms of liberalism, such as those found in society, economics, and politics.

Since modernity was committed to the idea that science explains all, *theological* liberals questioned anything that science could not prove. Science could not prove that God existed, so liberals reduced God to Friedrich Schleiermacher's "feeling of absolute dependence" (Schleiermacher 1999, p. 16) or Paul Tillich's "Ground of Being." (Tillich 1957, p. 7) Similarly, science could not prove that Jesus was God, so liberals declared that Jesus was merely the Son in a moral sense. He was only a human, but his complete reliance on the Ground of Being earned him the title "Son of God." Science taught that miracles and the resurrection are impossible, so modern theology generally reduced Jesus' miracles to moral lessons and his resurrection to an inspiring reminder that winter snow always leads to spring growth.

Besides their reliance upon the closed universe of modern science, theological liberals also thought they knew best about morality. They were confident that they knew what was right and what was wrong, and they expected God to conform to their principles of morality. So it didn't take long for them to challenge the biblical teaching on hell. They didn't care that in the Scriptures Jesus spoke more than anyone else about hell, or that every New Testament author taught the final punishment of the wicked (see Matt. 5:20–30; Mark 9:42–48; Luke 16:19–31; Paul—2 Thess. 1:5–10; Heb. 10:27–31; James 4:12; 5:1–5; 2 Peter 2:4–17; Jude 13–23; John—Rev. 11:14; 20: 10–15; 21:8; 22:15). These reasonable scholars were sure that a loving God would send only the very worst sinners to hell, and only for a while. Nineteenth-century Americans had finally turned from the evils of slavery, and they could not fathom that God would torture people—as they had done to slaves, only worse and forever. In the words of the Unitarian preacher William Channing, such ideas "fill our minds with a horror which we want [lack] words to express" (Channing, p. 377).

It is helpful to know something about liberal theology to understand what Bell is doing in *Love Wins*, for as Mark Galli explained in his review in *Christianity Today*, Bell's book belongs in the family of theological liberalism (Galli, p. 65). Bell's postmodern brand of liberalism differs in important ways from the modern variety—for instance, he has not denied the deity of Christ—but his reinterpretation of hell makes the liberal move of keeping biblical language while redefining what it means.

Deconstructing Hell

Bell clearly believes that a hell awaits unrepentant sinners when they die, but he doesn't seem to think that this suffering in the afterlife will be much worse than the earthly "hell" they presently experience. He writes that he believes "in a literal hell" because he has been to Rwanda and seen numerous teenagers whose arms and legs were chopped off in the horrific genocide in that country. He believes in hell because he has looked into the eyes of a drug addict, sat with a woman who was raped, groaned with a child whose father committed suicide, and counseled a family whose child was molested by a relative (pp. 70–72).

We don't have words to describe such horrific scenarios. We can say they are "awful," "dreadful," and "shocking," but these terms don't begin to cover our outrage. Who can read these stories and not weep for those who have suffered so much? But let's be clear: as unthinkably awful as these situations unmistakably are, they are not even close to the God-forsaken torment of hell. If the appalling mutilation of Rwandan children was comparable to hell, then why would Jesus say that it is better for us to mutilate ourselves than to be cast into hell? Jesus said, "If your right eye causes you to stumble, gouge it out and throw it away...And if your right hand causes you to sin, cut it off and throw it away. It is better for you to lose one part of your body than for your whole body to go into hell" (Matt. 5:29–30).

Bell explains that in this passage Jesus is merely warning people not to sinfully create their own hell. For example, writes Bell, an unrepentant man who cheats on his wife creates his own hell by destroying "their marriage and children and finances and friendships and future." This man realizes too late:

Gouging out his eye may actually have been a better choice.

Some agony needs agonizing language.
Some destruction does make you think of fire.
Some betrayal actually feels like you've been burned.
Some injustices do cause things to heat up. (p. 73)

This metaphorical and rather weak view of hell explains why *Love Wins* lacks the passionate pleas of Edwards—even if not expressed in the same searing language—to repent before it's too late. Based on a reading of *Love Wins*, one can scarcely imagine Bell imploring his congregation as Charles Haddon Spurgeon spoke to his church: "If sinners be damned, at least let them leap to hell over our bodies. And if they perish, let them perish with our arms about their knees, imploring them to stay. If hell must be filled, at least let it be filled in the teeth of our exertions, and let not one person go there unwarned and unprayed for" (Spurgeon, pp. 68–78).

The best appeal Bell musters appears near the end of *Love Wins*, when he warns that Jesus' "strong, shocking images of judgment and separation" mean that we might "miss out on rewards and celebrations and opportunities" (p. 197). Bell's language suggests that Jesus was the master of overkill, using "shocking images of judgment" merely to encourage people to come to his party. This version of Jesus doesn't sound like the God of love, but more like Jack Nicholson's sadistic Joker in *Batman*: "I really hope you can come to my fantastic party, because if you don't, I will have you thrown out into utter darkness and damnation".

Jesus' "shocking images of judgment" make sense only if Jesus was warning about a real and shocking judgment. Jesus surely meant more than Bell's observation that "people choose to live in their own hells all the time. We do it every time we isolate ourselves, give the cold shoulder to someone who has slighted us,…every time we harden our hearts in defiance of what we know to be the loving, good, and right thing to do" (p. 114).

Does Bell really intend to say that giving someone a cold shoulder is hell? Giving or receiving a cold shoulder may be annoying, but it certainly isn't worth gouging out an eye or sawing off an arm to avoid. If, as Bell says, the term "hell" is "a loaded, volatile, adequately violent, dramatic, serious word" (p. 93), then we should not use it for anything less than the lake of fiery judgment. Some words are so strong that it's offensive to use them in lighter scenarios. We're shocked when millionaire athletes compare their jobs to slavery, or when oblivious blowhards suggest that their injustice is their own personal "holocaust." Slavery and holocaust are loaded terms, and we must use them only to refer to real slavery and an actual holocaust. The same is true for hell, which is inconceivably worse.

Bell makes the same mistake with hell that he made with heaven in his previous chapter. There he assumed that our future heaven will not be much better than our present experience of heaven on earth, so here he suggests that the future hell will not be much worse than our own little hells we create. Remarkably, Bell's interpretation of the parable of the prodigal son suggests that heaven and hell are the same place! He states that both sons attended the same party thrown by their father, which was heaven for the prodigal son but hell for the selfish elder son. Bell concludes,

> Jesus puts the older brother right there at the party, but refusing to trust the father's version of his story. Refusing to join in the celebration.
>
> Hell is being at the party.
> That's what makes it so hellish. (p. 169)

Actually, Jesus was not telling his self-righteous listeners that their pride was the same thing as hell, but that if they continued in sin then they would end up in hell. Hell is the dreadful consequence of our sinful choices, not the choices themselves. Hell is not "our refusal to trust God's retelling of our story" (p. 170). Hell is what happens to us after we die if we don't trust and obey. *Love Wins* repeatedly minimizes the awfulness of hell. Hell ends up being not much worse than what sinners presently experience—and even if it is, they will have a way out.

Hell in the Bible

Bell bases his argument that sinners will be able to escape hell on several passages, none of which supports the argument. First, he believes that Ezekiel 16:53—which says that God "will restore the fortunes of Sodom"—means that every person who perished in Sodom's hail of fire and brimstone will be restored. But God was merely promising to restore the city, not every individual who ever dwelled there. Bell then cites Matthew 11:23–24, in which Jesus tells Capernaum that "it will be more bearable for Sodom on the day of judgment than for you." Bell concludes that "more bearable for Sodom" means "there's still hope" for Sodom, so every citizen of Sodom may yet be saved (pp. 84–85). This is an amazing claim, for not only does "more bearable" not mean "there's still hope," but it assumes that Sodom will be judged, just less severely than those cities which suppressed more light. Jesus is saying that Sodom and Capernaum will be judged, not that both will be saved.

Second, Bell pushes ahead with numerous promises from the Old Testament prophets that God will restore both his people and the pagan people of Egypt (p. 88). Bell assumes that such passages imply that every person who ever lived there will be able to leave hell. But the idea of escaping from hell never comes up in these passages. God is merely promising that those who call on the Lord in this life will be saved, and that, in fact, many will call on him.

Third, Bell mentions that Paul sometimes hands sinners over to Satan so they can learn their lesson and be restored (pp. 89–90; 1 Tim. 1:20; 1 Cor. 5:5). This is the purpose of church discipline—to allow the wayward sinner to hit bottom and awaken to their need for Jesus. But Paul gives no indication that these sinners did return to Christ or that they will have an opportunity to do so after they die.

Finally, Bell surprisingly appeals to the judgment of the sheep and the goats, a story which is often used to support everlasting punishment for the goats. In Matthew 25:46, Jesus invites the sheep into "eternal life" and sends the goats to "eternal punishment." Most biblical scholars believe that the goats' "eternal punishment" is indeed eternal, because the same term *aionion* is used for the sheep's eternal life. If *aionion* means that the sheep's life lasts forever, then to be consistent, it must also mean that the goats' punishment lasts forever. Presumably the goats also will suffer punishment, for they are cursed and cast "into the eternal fire prepared for the devil and his angels" (v. 41).

Despite the intuitive appeal of this traditional interpretation, Bell suggests that rather than suffer eternal punishment, the goats will actually experience only "a period of pruning," "a time of trimming," or "an intense experience of correction" (p. 91). He says this is one possible way to read the phrase *aion* of *kolazo* in Matthew 25:46. However, the Greek text does not actually say "*aion* of *kolazo*," but rather "*kolasin aionion.*"

Bell's phrase, "*aion of kolazo*," literally means "age of I punish/ prune." Unless we assume that Jesus' grammar was very poor, it's difficult to imagine him saying this. The phrase Jesus actually uses, "*kolasin aionion*," refers to a period of pruning or punishment that lasts longer than a single age, or *aion*. It lasts through all the ages, which is why Jesus uses the adjectival form *aionion*. Even if you don't know Greek, it's not hard to figure out that Jesus is speaking of "eternal punishment." As I mentioned above, the cursed goats are cast "into the eternal fire prepared for the devil and his angels" (v. 41). Unless "the devil and his angels" are heading to hell for a temporary time of correction, it's safe to assume that "eternal punishment" in verse 46 means what English Bibles say it means.

The Beginning of the End

Bell's diminished view of hell is not an isolated argument. Scholars disagree whether the liberal dismissal of hell is the start of a slippery slope or whether it is a sign that the ground of faith has already shifted, but either way it's obvious that one's view on hell is inextricably tied up with other doctrines. For starters, it is difficult to reject the finality of hell and hold a high view of Scripture, for the Bible repeatedly says that unbelievers "will be punished with everlasting destruction" (2 Thess. 1:9). As Bell points out, one's view of hell also has implications for one's view of God. Can God be loving if he sends anyone to hell? Can he be just if he doesn't? If God never condemns any unrepentant sinner to hell forever, then has his love become nothing more than sentimentality—what disobedient children wish their parents were like?

Jettisoning hell also demands that we reassess the sinfulness of humanity. If we say that a loving God would never send anyone to hell forever, we are already assuming that no one deserves to stay there. Bell makes this point repeatedly in *Love Wins*. He writes, "Have billions of people been created only to spend eternity in conscious punishment and torment, suffering infinitely for the finite sins they committed in the few years they spent on earth?" (p. 102). Bell writes often and eloquently about the sins we commit against each other and the earth, but *Love Wins* is silent about how our sin might offend a holy God.

After it ratchets human sinfulness down, this modern view of hell goes to work on the atonement. If we are not *that* sinful, then it doesn't make sense that Jesus had to bear the penalty for our sin on the cross. And so Bell concludes that the "sacrificial metaphor" of Christ's blood being shed for us no longer resonates in our modern world. He explains, "But we don't live any longer in a culture in which people offer animal sacrifices to the gods. People did live that way for thousands of years, and there are pockets of primitive cultures around the world that do continue to understand sin, guilt, and atonement in those ways. But most of us don't" (pp. 128–29).

If the sacrificial "metaphor" is outdated for us, then what exactly was Jesus doing for us on the cross? All liberals can say is that Jesus was merely leaving us an example to follow. He was simply showing us how to trust our Father in our darkest hour; how to resist the social evils of religious bigotry, political graft, class contempt, and mob rule; or how to serve others and forgive our enemies. According to Bell, the cross is "a reminder, a sign, a glimpse, an icon that allows us to tap into our deepest longings to be part of a new creation" (p. 137). The cross reveals that Jesus "is the source, the strength, the example, and the assurance that this pattern of death and rebirth is the way into the only kind of life that actually sustains and inspires" (p. 136).

Of course, Jesus can inspire us to follow his example without being God, so the next logical step for liberalism is to deny the unique deity of Jesus Christ. I am not saying that Bell himself has taken this step, only that this is the next move that liberals historically have made. They often claim to believe in the deity of Christ, because that is what the creeds say, but they dumb down the doctrine until it means virtually nothing. As W. Robertson Smith exclaimed when told that some were saying he denied the deity of Christ, "How can they accuse me of that? I've never denied the divinity of any man, let alone Jesus" (cited in Erickson, p 758).

Finally, if Jesus is not God, it doesn't take long for modern theological liberals to begin wondering if they still need to think about God in the traditional way. Christians have always believed that God is a distinct being who is separate from his creation, but liberals often assert that God is nothing more than the force which runs through the universe. Many liberals opt for a form of panentheism, where "God" is merely the sum total of everything in the universe. He becomes "the One," "the Whole," and "the Ground of Being" rather than the transcendent, triune, and personal God of the Bible.

It's hard to tell where Bell falls on this question, as he seems to say that God is both a being and a force. He asks,

> Is there a force, an energy, a being calling out to us,
> in many languages, using a variety of methods and events,
> trying to get our attention?" (p. 141)

He writes, "There is an energy in the world, a spark, an electricity that everything is plugged into. The Greeks called it *zoe*, the mystics call it 'Spirit,' and Obi-Wan called it 'the Force.'" This "energy that gives life to everything is called the 'Word of God,'" and it is this "life-giving 'Word of God'" which "took on flesh and blood" (pp. 144–46). I'm not sure I understand what Bell is saying here, but if he means that the deity of Jesus is nothing more than a divine energy that resides within Christ, then he has committed the liberal error of reinterpreting the deity of Christ to make it palatable to modern (or postmodern) ears. And that would be a denial of Jesus' deity, as traditionally understood.

When we reinterpret the biblical teaching on hell, we inevitably redefine everything else we believe. I am not saying that Bell has reached the bottom of the slippery slope to liberalism, but there are signs that his reassessment is already underway.

Conclusion

Like other theological liberals, Bell reinterprets Scripture's stern warnings about hell until they fit the modern idea of what a loving God must do. And so he produces an indulgent, nonjudgmental God who sounds exactly like the god of popular culture.

This is the Achilles' heel of theological liberalism. The culture may be initially attracted to the liberal gospel of human reason and individual autonomy—finally we have a group of Christians who get it!—but soon enough, people realize that this weak-kneed version of Christianity is simply redundant. Most people think that they are basically good—certainly good enough to earn their way into heaven, though they probably should try harder to love their neighbor. This is essentially the liberal message, with Jesus thrown in for morally good but not biblically sound measure.

Eventually the broader culture realizes that liberal churches are not saying anything that hasn't already been said a hundred times on *Oprah*. So why bother telling the "Jesus story"? They logically ask, "If Jesus is nothing more than the way Christians talk about loving their neighbor, then why can't we love our neighbor without the Jesus talk?" And so liberal churches decline, for people won't make the effort to get up and go to church when they can sleep in and hear the same moral and uplifting message on television. As C. S. Lewis reminded his friend, "Did you ever meet, or hear of, anyone who was converted from scepticism to a 'liberal' or 'demythologised' Christianity? I think that when unbelievers come in at all, they come in a good deal further" (Lewis 2002, p. 119).

But what if unbelievers don't have to come in? What if everyone—good and bad, Christian or not—is ultimately saved in the end? This is the question of universalism, and it is the subject of the next chapter.

Universalism

5

Is Rob Bell a universalist? This question has sparked most of the controversy over *Love Wins*. In fact, if you have picked up my book because you read *Love Wins*, there is a good chance you opened to this chapter first. You'll learn more from this chapter if you read the earlier chapters first, but if you insist on plowing ahead you'll still be able to get the gist of universalism and whether or not Bell fits that label.

Universalism is the belief that everyone will be saved in the end. Regardless of what they believed or how they behaved, everyone ultimately will be reconciled to God. This is an extremely positive message, and some may wonder why anyone would argue against it. What kind of grump would say that God doesn't empty hell and save everyone? Are evangelicals, in particular, that miserly about eternal life?

Evangelicals oppose universalism because we believe that Scripture clearly teaches that some people will go to hell forever. For instance, consider the angel's stern warning in Revelation 14:9–11:

If anyone worships the beast and its image and receives
its mark on their forehead or on their hand, they, too, will
drink the wine of God's fury, which has been poured full
strength into the cup of his wrath. They will be tormented
with burning sulfur in the presence of the holy angels and
of the Lamb. And the smoke of their torment will rise for
ever and ever. There will be no rest day or night for those
who worship the beast and its image, or for anyone who
receives the mark of its name.

It would be difficult to reconcile this passage with universalism, or even with a second chance for postmortem salvation.

Of course evangelicals want all people to be saved, but we
dare not promise universal salvation without a word from God.
Otherwise we would become modern Hananiahs, imitators of
the false prophet who wrongly told rebellious Judah that God
had told him all would be well. Jeremiah confronted Hana-
niah, "The LORD has not sent you, yet you have persuaded this
nation to trust in lies. Therefore this is what the LORD says: 'I
am about to remove you from the face of the earth. This very
year you are going to die'" (Jer. 28:15–16). Apparently God
takes very seriously how others use or abuse his Word. He is
angry with those who spread false hope, who claim to speak
for him when he has not spoken.

This biblical reason would be enough to oppose universalism, but many also think that it forfeits the urgency
of repentance and faith. If someone believed that they had
forever to make peace with God, why would they bother
to do it now? And why would they urgently implore others
to do it now? Universalists don't concede that they lack
enthusiasm for evangelism—they say it's exciting to inform

people that they are going to be okay. But the fact is that if everyone is saved in the end, they ultimately don't need to know it now.

Varieties of Universalism

Before we examine Bell's views, it seems helpful to briefly sketch the most popular forms of universalism in church history. This will enable us to see where Bell fits historically, which in turn will help us to more precisely identify and evaluate his position. There have been two dominant forms of universalism, one which relies on an enduring belief in *human freedom* and one which focuses on *God's freedom*.

1. Origen and human freedom

Origen was a third-century church father who learned Neoplatonism from our old friend, Ammonius Saccas. Neoplatonism's belief in the superiority of the spiritual world led Origen to allegorize Scripture (looking beyond the literal words to a higher, spiritual meaning) and to live a rigidly ascetic existence. Origen treated his body so harshly that rumors circulated that he had emasculated himself after reading Jesus' words that some men became eunuchs for the sake of the kingdom (Matt. 19:12). Historians believe that these rumors were started by Origen's enemies, for Origen was famously committed to the allegorical interpretation of Scripture. How sad if the one verse he took literally was that one!

Origen's theology begins with the assumption that people have free choice. But he also observed that to some extent people's fate is determined by their lot in life. Some people are smarter or stronger than others, which seems to give them an unfair advantage. Origen was additionally troubled by

Paul's statement that God loved Jacob but hated Esau (Rom. 9). There must be a reason for this, but what?

Origen solved this puzzle by asserting that everyone earned their present condition by how far they fell in a previous life. He said that all created personal beings started out as disembodied souls in the presence of God, but they became so satiated with the glory of God that their love for him cooled and they turned to inferior things. God punished their disobedience by placing them in this world. The souls that sinned the most became demons, the souls that sinned the least became angels, and the ones that sinned moderately became humans, trapped in the prison of their physical bodies. Origen believed that this world is a training ground to lead us back to God, and that God would continue to reincarnate our souls into new, successive worlds until every soul made it all the way back. Origen famously said that even the devil eventually could be saved, a point which contributed to his posthumous condemnation by the Second Council of Constantinople (553 CE).

It's important to note that Origen believed that souls never lost their freedom to choose. Even after every soul had been reconciled to God it was entirely possible that they might fall away, prompting God to start the whole process over again. Origen's emphasis on freedom held out hope for a universal salvation, but it also meant that no salvation would be final.

2. Barth and divine freedom

I don't think you can persuasively argue for universalism from Scripture, but if you were going to be a universalist, you couldn't do better than the Swiss theologian Karl Barth

(1886–1968). Barth is wrong to be a universalist, but at least he has a good reason.

Barth was a Reformed theologian who began from the assumption of sovereign grace. He declared that if God is all-loving and all-powerful, then we might expect God to exert his power and lovingly brush aside our sin and save us anyway. We may say no to God, but our puny rejection stands no chance against God's overpowering YES toward us. Barth's theology is more complex than I can explain here, but you can see how his emphasis on God's loving sovereignty might inspire some exciting preaching.

Barth often reminded his audience that their sinful rebellion was powerless to resist the overwhelming force of God's love:

> He can become a sinner and place himself within the shadow of divine judgment…He does all this. But he cannot reverse or change the eternal decision of God…Man can certainly keep on lying (and does so); but he cannot make truth falsehood. He can certainly rebel (he does so); but he can accomplish nothing which abolishes the choice of God. He can certainly flee from God (he does so); but he cannot escape Him. He can certainly hate God and be hateful to God (he does and is so); but he cannot change into its opposite the eternal love of God which triumphs even in his hate…He may let go of God, but God does not let go of him. (Barth 1957, p. 317)

Barth believed that we are powerless to resist God because ultimately our choices don't count. He argued that Jesus is the first and only true human (Barth's counting differs from Rom. 5:12–21, which says that Adam was the first man), so whatever is true about Jesus' life is also true about every other human person. Barth said that Jesus was rejected by God when he died and descended into hell, but that Jesus was subsequently elected and rescued by God when the Father raised him from the dead. Since Jesus is the first human, and every human derives from and is in him, what happened to Jesus also happened (and continues happening) to everyone. Most people are unaware that they have risen with Jesus, so the task of Christian missions is to spread the good news that everyone is already saved.

Barth's emphasis on the centrality of Christ and the freedom of God led him to the brink of universalism, but he refused to step over the edge. He would not say for sure that God would save everyone, for he feared that committing God to universal salvation would compromise God's sovereignty. How could God be genuinely free if a human being knew what God must do? So Barth said that God was free enough to veto our human rebellion, but also free enough to permit it to stand. He suspected that God would do the former, but he would not guarantee it. This is why Barth is often called an "incipient universalist" (see Hesselink, p. 115). He boldly implied that the God "who loves in freedom" would disregard our sin and save everyone, but he was too careful a theologian to say for sure.

Barth's theology is attractive, but his incipient universalism suffers from two main problems: it lacks a sufficient base in Scripture (Barth employs a clever but idiosyncratic interpretation of Scripture), and it eliminates human freedom. Ultimately it doesn't matter whether we ever choose Christ, either in this life or in the next. All that matters is what happened to Jesus. Barth's system completely discounts the importance of our own, human choices, and for this reason most people who are attracted to universalism opt for a version of Origen's human-centered freedom.

Why Rob Bell Is(n't) a Universalist

1. Why Bell is a universalist

Bell seems to be a universalist for the same reason as Karl Barth. He claims that if God is all-powerful and all-loving, then he must want to save everyone and must be powerful enough to pull it off. Bell's title for chapter four, "Does God Get What God Wants?," indicates how Bell intends to argue for some type of universalism. Bell pokes fun at traditional Christians who say that God wants everyone to be saved but just can't get it done. "How great is God?" Bell asks rhetorically.

> Great enough to achieve what God sets out to do,
> or kind of great,
> medium great,
> great most of the time,
> but in this,
> the fate of billions of people,
> not totally great. [*sic*]
> Sort of great.
> A little great. (pp. 97–98)

Bell suggests that this traditional God, who lacks the power to save everyone, will have to settle for what he can realistically achieve. In the end, Bell speculates, this impotent God will have to shrug and say,

Well, I tried, I gave it my best shot,
and sometimes you just have to be okay with failure. (p. 103)

The center of Bell's chapter on universalism throws a lengthy bouquet in its direction. He writes that not only is the Christian faith "big enough, wide enough, and generous enough" to make room for universalism (p. 110), but also universalism has been "at the center of the Christian tradition since the first church" (p. 109). Actually, this is historically incorrect. There have always been stray universalists popping up here and there, mostly in the East and mostly enormously influenced by Plato. Every name that Bell lists as a universalist (p. 107) belongs to the philosophical family of Origen (except Clement, who anticipated and influenced Origen's thought). But this Origen school is the exception which proves the rule: the center, circumference, and everything in between of the Christian tradition have always held that some people unfortunately end up in hell.

Bell's slippery grasp of history appears again in his selective quotation from Martin Luther. Bell observes that Luther once wrote to a friend concerning the possibility of postmortem salvation, "Who would doubt God's ability to do that?" (p. 106). And so Bell concludes that even Luther was open to the possibility of a second chance for salvation. But Bell overlooks Luther's very next words: "No one, however, can prove that he does do this. For all that we read is that he has already raised people from the dead and thus granted them faith. But whether he gives faith or not, *it is impossible for anyone to be saved without faith*. Otherwise every sermon, the gospel, and faith would be vain, false, and deceptive, since the *entire gospel makes faith necessary*" (Luther 1968, pp. 53–54; italics added).

Like other late medieval theologians, Luther distinguished between God's absolute power and his ordained power. God's *absolute power* could do absolutely anything: it could create a world without gravity, send the Messiah through the Chinese race, or save people even after they die. But God's *ordained power* is how he has chosen to act, and it makes things what they are. So while God's absolute power could hypothetically do anything, God's ordained power chooses to create gravity, send Jesus as a Jew, and save those who put their faith in his Son. Thus, the letter that Bell quotes actually argues that faith is necessary for salvation. Luther did not endorse postmortem salvation or universalism.

Despite this faulty historical ground, Bell argues that universalism is a better story than the traditional view "in which billions of people spend forever somewhere in the universe trapped in a black hole of endless torment and misery with no way out" (p. 110). Bell is careful not to unequivocally endorse universalism, but he clearly admires its belief that "given enough time, everybody will turn to God and find themselves in the joy and peace of God's presence. The love of God will melt every hard heart, and even the most 'depraved sinners' will eventually give up their resistance and turn to God" (p. 107). He agrees with universalism's premise that "no one can resist God's pursuit forever," and he affirms its conclusion: "Restoration brings God glory; eternal torment doesn't. Reconciliation brings God glory; endless anguish doesn't. Renewal and return cause God's greatness to shine through the universe; never-ending punishment doesn't" (p. 108).

Finally, Bell cites numerous biblical passages which indicate that the whole world will return to God (p. 99). We evangelicals join Bell in joyful anticipation of the day when "all people will come" to God (Ps. 65:2), when "the nations will know that I am the LORD" (Ezek. 36:23), and "all the ends of the earth will see the salvation of our God" (Isa. 52:10). But as I mentioned in chapter two, these passages do not mean, nor do they imply, that every last person who has ever lived will be saved. The apostle Paul promises that one day "every knee [shall] bow…and every tongue acknowledge that Jesus Christ is Lord" (Phil. 2:10–11), but there is no indication that such tardy worship will result in salvation. Instead, Paul declares that those who in this life "do not know God and do not obey the gospel of our Lord Jesus…will be punished with everlasting destruction" (2 Thess. 1:8–9).

2. Why Bell isn't a universalist

Bell's emphasis on God's loving freedom follows Barth's example and pushes hard in the direction of universalism. And like Barth, Bell also stops just short of committing to full-blown universalism. But the reason Bell gives for stopping on the brink doesn't come from Barth, but from Origen. Barth wouldn't promise universal salvation because he thought it compromised *God's freedom*; Bell won't promise universal salvation because he believes it compromises *our freedom*.

Bell explains that true love must be free, and freedom requires options. God cannot take our options away and compel us to love him, for "if at any point God overrides, co-opts, or hijacks the human heart, robbing us of our freedom to choose, then God has violated the fundamental essence of what love even is" (p. 104). And so Bell concludes, "Love demands freedom. It always has, and it always will. We are free to resist, reject, and rebel against God's ways for us. We can have all the hell we want" (p. 113). Again,

God gives us what we want, and if that's hell, we can have it. We have that kind of freedom, that kind of choice. We are that free. (p. 72)

Bell's emphasis on human freedom prevents him from becoming a full-fledged universalist. He does allow for the possibility that someone will reject God's love and choose to remain in hell. However, it seems fair to call Bell, as with Barth, an "incipient universalist." His view may not check all the boxes on the universalist membership card, but it leans strongly in that direction. Bell apparently believes that it's unlikely that any mere human will be able to outlast the omnipotent God, who "never stops pursuing," who "simply doesn't give up. Ever" (p. 101).

I also think it's fair to call Bell a "functional universalist," for one undeniable takeaway from *Love Wins* is that everyone who desires to leave hell will be able to do so. Bell leaves open the possibility that someone may choose to remain in hell, but I doubt that many of his readers think that will be them. Presumably anyone who accepts Bell's argument will also likely believe that they will choose God in the end. And so there is no practical difference between full-on universalism and Bell's "functional" or "incipient" kind. All varieties leave the firm impression that no one needs to worry much about hell—even if there is one.

Unresolved Problems

Bell's unique blend of Barth and Origen leaves him with deep problems in his understanding of both God and salvation. First, Bell opens chapter four with nine pages that ridicule the traditional view of God. How can Christians say their God is great when he can't even get what he wants? What kind of weak God wants to save everyone and then miserably fails? Bell forcefully answers that his view of God is better than that, for he believes that God's love "is stronger and more powerful" than "the hardness of the human heart" (p. 109). His God will undoubtedly get whatever God wants.

Or will he? Bell begins backpedaling when he introduces the variable of human freedom. It turns out that Bell's God respects our freedom too much to compel us to love him. Indeed, God may not always get what God wants. At this point you might expect Bell to apologize to those who hold the traditional view, since his understanding of God suffers from the same problem as theirs. Instead, he simply changes the question:

> Now back to that original question: 'Does God get what God wants?' is a good question, an interesting question, an important question that gives us much to discuss.
>
> But there's a better question...
> . . . .
> It's not "Does God get what God wants?"
> but
> "Do we get what we want?"
>
> And the answer to that is a resounding, affirming, sure, and positive yes.
> Yes, we get what we want.
>
> God is that loving." (pp. 116–18)

Even more remarkable, Bell concludes the chapter by declaring that our freedom to reject God is a gift of God's love:

> If we want hell,
> if we want heaven,
> they are ours.
> That's how love works. It can't be forced, manipulated, or coerced.
> It always leaves room for the other to decide.
> God says yes,
> we can have what we want,
> because love wins. (pp. 118–19)

According to Bell, when evangelicals say that God gives humans the freedom to reject him and then live with the consequences of those actions, the result is a "devastating" and "psychologically crushing" God who is impossible to love (pp. 174–75). But when Bell's God gives people freedom to reject him and then live with the consequences, "love wins"? It's unclear to me why one God is "terrifying and traumatizing and unbearable" (p. 175) and the other one is the greatest example of love.

Since Bell's understanding of God seems to face the same dilemma as the traditional view, his argument would benefit from an important distinction that the traditional view uses to talk about God. Theologians have long distinguished between God's hidden, sovereign will and his revealed, moral will. God's sovereign will includes whatever happens in our world, whether good or bad. We don't have access to this will before events unfold, but we take comfort in knowing that whatever comes our way has been allowed by God (Eph. 1:11). We are responsible for God's revealed will, which, among other things, tells us that God wants all to be saved (1 Tim. 2:4). We finite creatures cannot comprehend how God wants everyone to be saved and yet sovereignly allows people to reject him and choose hell. But we believe that Scripture teaches both, and so, as even Bell concedes, we choose to leave this tension unresolved (p. 115).

Second, Bell's universalism leaves people deeply insecure about their own salvation. He charges that the traditional view of hell leaves us in a fearful state. "Is history tragic?" he asks.

> Is our future uncertain,
> or will God take care of us?
> Are we safe?
> Are we secure?
> Or are we on our own? (p. 102)

Bell seems to think that his perspective gives us reason to feel secure, but actually his emphasis on human freedom means that our salvation is never final, never guaranteed by God.

Origen taught that the fact that we never lose our freedom means that even when every soul has returned to God, we may choose to fall away and need to be saved all over again. Bell's view suffers from the same problem, for he declares that the open gates of heaven mean that "people are free to come and go" (p. 115). If we are free to go, then we may eventually lose our love for God and choose to walk out of heaven. Bell writes that we can reject "our God-given goodness and humanity…anytime, anywhere, with anyone" (p. 73), and I presume that would also include heaven. Bell does not address this possibility, but it is clearly implied in both his and Origen's focus on human freedom.

It is precisely this instability of human freedom that led Martin Luther to praise the security of God's grace. In a transparent paragraph in *The Bondage of the Will*, Luther explained that if salvation was put in his hands he would surely drop it. "But now, since God has taken my salvation out of my hands into his, making it depend on his choice and not mine, and has promised to save me, not by my own work or exertion but by his grace and mercy, I am assured and certain both that he is faithful and will not lie to me, and also that he is too great and powerful for any demons or any adversities to be able to break him or to snatch me from him" (Luther 2005, p. 193).

Luther knew that true security can be found only in God. It doesn't help a trembling sinner to hear that the vast majority of the human race will likely choose God. What if he is one of the few who don't? Or what if she does now but may later change her mind? People who understand the depth of their depravity know all too well that this could be them. They don't trust their own freedom, but only the sure, strong hands of God. They contentedly curl up in God's hands of grace, confident that he will not drop them.

Conclusion

So is Bell a universalist? Yes and no. He seems to side with Barth's emphasis on the overwhelming force of God's love, yet he accepts Origen's premise that human freedom is ultimately unpredictable. I think it's fair to say that Bell is an "incipient universalist" like Barth, but for Origen's reason.

Bell doesn't seem to notice that Origen's focus on human freedom produces a latent insecurity in his view of salvation.

Perhaps Bell overlooks this because he thinks that it's relatively easy to resist sin and choose God. This raises the question, how sinful does Bell think we are? What does he think we need to be saved from? I will examine this critically important subject next.

Sin

6

Early in the fifth century, a British monk named Pelagius became enraged as a bishop in Rome read this prayer from St. Augustine's *Confessions*: "O Charity, my God, set me on fire! You command continence: grant what you command, and command what you will" (Augustine 1991, p. 202).

This is precisely our problem, Pelagius fumed. We humans talk as if we can't keep God's commands on our own. We know what God expects from us, and yet "we shout in God's face and say, 'It's hard! It's difficult! We can't! We are but men, encompassed by the frailty of the flesh!'" (see Stevenson, p. 234). We tell God that we are unable to be chaste and holy, and that if he wants us to live that way he is going to have to accomplish it himself. So we sit around and wait for God to give us what he commands, becoming lazier and more sinful all the while.

Pelagius's view sounds like a commonsense approach to tough love. God won't do for us what we can do for ourselves, or as Ben Franklin put it in *Poor Richard's Almanac*, "God helps those who help themselves" (see Augustyn, p. 37). Many Christians mistakenly think that these words appear in the Bible. Well, surprise! Not only are these words not biblical, but a century after Augustine had finished with Pelagius, the Western church agreed at the Second Council of Orange that Pelagians weren't even Christian (see McGrath 2007, pp. 425–6).

In this chapter I present Pelagius' views on sin and grace as expressed in his polemical battle with Augustine. My point here is not that Augustine won and Pelagius lost, but rather that the church through history has repeatedly affirmed the Augustinian side of many similar debates about human nature, sin, and grace. So it makes sense to examine *Love Wins* in the light of this biblical, historical understanding of the Christian faith. Once it is clear why the church deemed Pelagius' position to be outside the bounds of Christian orthodoxy, I will examine whether the views expressed in *Love Wins* commit the age-old Pelagian mistake, and if so, to what extent.

Pelagianism

Pelagius defended his view in his book *On Nature*, to which Augustine responded with his *On Nature and Grace*. I will first present Pelagius' position, and then explain how Augustine argued that his perspective lacked enough grace to be Christian.

1. Pelagius' *On Nature*

Pelagius assumed that human nature was good and unbroken by sin. He knew that we often do bad things, but he blamed this on our environment. We sin because we imitate the bad examples of others. This superficial view of sin led Pelagius to argue that we possess the power to stop sinning anytime we choose. He said that God gave us the ability to do what is right, and now it is up to us to use that capacity both to will and to do it. God supplies the ability, but we have to supply the will and the act. Pelagius believed that we never lose this God-given ability to will and to do what is right. Nothing, not even sin, can take away our free choice. We are free to love and obey God anytime we want.

Pelagius illustrated his position by comparing our ability to obey God with our natural abilities of sight and locomotion. God has given us eyes and legs, but it is up to us to look and to walk. Just as we wouldn't sit around with our eyes closed, praying to God that we might walk and see, so we should not sit on our hands and pretend that we are unable to please God. If we want to see, we must open our eyes. If we want to walk, we must stand up and move. And if we want to please God, we must rise and obey.

Pelagius' light view of sin led him to a corresponding light view of grace. If our natures are not in too much trouble—if we retain the ability to do what is right whenever we want— then it stands to reason that we don't need *that* much help from God. Pelagius believed that we need God's forgiveness for past sin, but in the present all we need from him is what he has already supplied. God has given us a good nature—a sound mind, a free will, and a sensitive conscience to guide us. He has also granted us his commands in Scripture, so we know precisely what he expects from us, and he has given us the example of Christ, so we know how to do what he commands. Our healthy natures and the teaching of Scripture are all God needs to give us, and it's all he is going to give us. If, after all that, we're still not holy, we can only blame ourselves.

2. Augustine's *On Nature and Grace*

Augustine agreed that it's our fault when we sin, but he didn't think that implied that we possess the ability to stop sinning whenever we want. Augustine argued that sin—first Adam's sin and then our own—has so corrupted our nature that we have lost the ability to will and to do what is right. To use Pelagius' analogies of sight and locomotion, sin has blinded our eyes and paralyzed our legs. Just as it's futile to implore a blind man to see and a lame man to walk, so it's useless to tell sinners that they have the ability to please God if they only want to badly enough. Augustine said that our broken natures must be healed before we can obey. We need God's medicine of full and complete grace.

Augustine observed that while Pelagius used the term "grace"—because that's how Christians talk—Pelagius' notion of grace meant little more than nature. Pelagius said that God graces us by giving us a healthy nature, the commands of Scripture, and the example of Christ. While Augustine was thankful for all of these, he said that rebellious sinners need even more. What good is it to talk about free choice if our wills are bound by sin? We won't freely choose what is right unless God first repairs our depraved (or "corrupt") wills. Augustine concluded that we need more than the external encouragement and examples of Scripture. We need an internal operation of God whereby the Holy Spirit miraculously and mysteriously opens our eyes, heals our spiritual legs, and makes us willing and able to love God. We need more than mere nature; we need both our nature *and* grace.

Augustine did not deny humans' personal responsibility. He agreed that if we are going to love God then *we* must do the loving. But he was realistic about what fallen sinners could do

Augustine vs Pelagius

on their own, apart from God. We *must* do it, but we *can't* do it, unless God first moves to heal our hearts and then empowers us all the way through the act of love. Augustine often quoted Philippians 2:12–13, which declares that it is precisely God's internal initiative which grounds our human responsibility. "Continue to work out your salvation with fear and trembling," wrote the apostle Paul, "for it is God who works in you to will and to act in order to fulfill his good purpose." Or as Augustine expressed it, "Give what you command, and then command whatever you will" (1997, p. 263).

In case you are (rightly) more impressed with Scripture than with theologians, please note that Augustine's view is thoroughly grounded in the Bible. For instance, consider Ephesians 2:1–10, which declares that when God found us we were completely unable to save ourselves. Paul says that we were "dead in [our] transgressions and sins...gratifying the cravings of our flesh and following its desires and thoughts. Like the rest, we were by nature deserving of wrath." But God mercifully took the initiative. He "made us alive with Christ even when we were dead in transgressions—it is by grace you have been saved." And so Paul concludes with the linchpin of Augustine's argument: we are saved "by grace...through faith—and this is not from yourselves, it is the gift of God— not by works, so that no one can boast." Finally, Paul explains that God's grace does not turn us into passive sinners—what Pelagius feared—but empowers us "in Christ Jesus to do good works, which God prepared in advance for us to do."

Near the beginning of *On Nature and Grace*, Augustine makes a stunning charge which will frame my discussion in this chapter: if Pelagius is correct that our human natures can obey God's commands without the need of grace, then it follows, wrote Augustine, that "Christ has died in vain" (Augustine 1997, p. 272; also see Gal. 2:21). Who needs Jesus if we can essentially save ourselves—if we can "work out" our salvation without God's own work in us? This chapter examines the first part of Augustine's charge: does *Love Wins* proclaim enough grace to be considered a Christian treatise—as the church historically has understood such sufficiency from the apostle Paul, through the Pelagian challenges, right up to today? In the following chapter I will examine the second part of Augustine's claim: if *Love Wins* is more Pelagian than Christian, then has its Jesus died for nothing?

Is *Love Wins* Pelagian?

The contrast between Pelagius and Augustine becomes clear if we think in terms of problem and solution. Pelagius had a shallow view of our problem—we suffer either from ignorance as we follow bad examples, or from a lazy selfishness that refuses to do what is right even when we know better. Pelagius' shallow problem required only an equally shallow solution—education that can defeat our ignorance and a steely determination that can conquer our sloth. We never lose our freedom of choice, so we can turn our lives around whenever we desire. MP of Pelagim.

Augustine believed that every person's problem was much more serious. He thought that we suffered from a sinful nature whose rebellion went all the way down, deep into the core of our being. We don't merely commit bad actions; we possess depraved characters which inevitably practice evil. Augustine argued that our deep problem required an equally invasive solution. First, it required the death of God's Son, for Jesus broke Satan's evil power when he bore our sin and its penalty in our place on the cross. Second, it required the death of our own sinful natures. As Augustine saw the solution, the Holy Spirit must change us from the inside out, compelling us to put our faith in the death and resurrection of God's Son.

Which of these models of sin and salvation—Pelagius' or Augustine's—is expressed in *Love Wins*?

1. Ignorance solved by enlightenment

For starters, it's evident that Bell thinks our main problem is ignorance. And this isn't too big a problem, for what we are ignorant of is the fact that we are already saved. Bell's assumption that we're already okay might explain why he begins his book by winking at the various ways the Bible allegedly says we could be saved. He asks,

> Is it what you say,
> or who you are,
> or what you do,
> or what you say you're going to do,
> or who your friends are,
> or who you're married to,
> or whether you give birth to children?
> Or is it what questions you're asked?
> Or is it what questions you ask in return?
> Or is it whether you do what you're told and go into the city? (pp. 16–17)

This opening hailstorm of questions might worry a person who desperately wants to know how to be saved. Such a reader might be asking: "Which way is it?" "How will I know?" "Can *anyone* tell me how to be saved!" These questions can be tossed out flippantly by someone who thinks that "how to be saved" is a bad question to begin with. A reader might initially think that Bell is presenting this flurry of irreconcilable questions to set us up for a later discussion on the real, ultimate answer to "What must a person do to be saved?" However, a major premise of *Love Wins* is that we don't need to be saved or do anything to enter the family of God, for we're already in the family simply because we're human.

Bell uses the story of the prodigal son to make the point that everyone—whether they are the "good" elder son or the "bad" prodigal son—is still God's child. Every human person—Christian and non-Christian alike—has God as their Father. Bell says that "we're all part of the same family" (p. 99), though many people don't yet realize this. Like the prodigal, they mistakenly think their sin has separated them from God. Bell explains:

> The younger brother believes that he is cut off, estranged, and no longer deserves to be his father's son, because of all the terrible things he's done.
>
> His badness is his problem, he thinks.
>
> …He is convinced that his destructive deeds have put him in such a bad state that he doesn't even *deserve* to be called a son anymore. (p. 185; italics original)

But Bell argues that the prodigal is mistaken. When he returns home, the prodigal discovers that he has never stopped being his father's son and that nothing he could ever do would remove him from his family. Bell says that the prodigal must

Jesus, "Repent for the Kingdom of God is at hand."
My sheep know my voice and I call unto them & they follow me.

choose whether to believe his own toxic story about his unworthiness or his father's forgiving story of love.

> He has to choose which one he will live in.
> Which one he will believe.
> Which one he will trust. (p. 166)

The solution to our problem of ignorance is a type of information we could call "enlightenment"—which is apparently why Bell wrote his book. He wants his readers to know that no "sins of the past" or "secrets that have been buried for years" can change

> the sure and certain truth that we are loved.
> That in spite of whatever has gone horribly wrong deep
> in our hearts
> and has spread to every corner of the world,
> in spite of our sins,
> failures,
> rebellion,
> and hard hearts,
> in spite of what's been done to us or what we've done,
>
> *God has made peace with us.*
>
> *Done. Complete.*
> As Jesus said, "It is finished." (pp. 171–72; italics added)

God has saved us

> before we could be good enough or right enough,

before we could even believe the right things.

Forgiveness is unilateral.

. . . .

God has already done it. (p. 189)

Unlike the apostle Paul, who said that Jesus made "peace through his blood, shed on the cross" (Col. 1:20)—a peace that we receive only when "we have been justified through faith" in him (Rom. 5:1)—Bell suggests that God is at peace with us simply because we are human. Remarkably, Bell cites Jesus' words in John 14:6—"No one comes to the Father except through me"—to argue that no one has to come to Jesus at all. Instead, Jesus is merely declaring "that he, and he alone, is saving everybody," whether they know it or not. He "simply claims that whatever God is doing in the world to know and redeem and love and restore the world is happening through him" (pp. 154–55). Thus, rather than fear the wrath of God against us and our sin (cf. John 3:36), we need only learn "to trust that we are loved" so that we can "say yes to this love of God, again and again and again" (pp. 194–95). And we probably don't need to worry if we don't come around in this life, for as the universalists say, there will be "endless opportunities in an endless amount of time for people to say yes to God" in the next one (pp. 106–7).

Since everyone is already in the family, whether they know it or not, Bell claims that evangelism is not about "entrance" into the kingdom of God but simply about its "enjoyment." He writes that Christians who focus on how to enter heaven "don't throw very good parties," and they tend "to cut people off from the explosive, liberating experience of the God who is an endless giving circle of joy and creativity" (pp. 178–79). Their "entrance understanding of the gospel rarely creates good art. Or innovation. Or a number of other things. It's a cheap view of the world, because it's a cheap view of God. It's a shriveled imagination" (pp. 179–80).

Conversely, those who don't worry about how to "get into heaven" but are simply content to enjoy their life with God—they are the ones who winsomely share their joy with others. Bell explains,

> God is love,
> and love *is* a relationship.
> This relationship is one of joy, and it can't be contained.
> (p. 178)

When you've experienced this universal and unconditional love of Christ, "you can't help but talk about him. You've tapped into the joy that fills the entire universe, and so naturally you want others to meet this God. This is a God worth telling people about" (p. 181).

I don't want to become distracted from the main point of this chapter, but I must respond briefly to Bell's unsupported claim that people who hold his view throw better parties and create higher forms of art than those who believe that people must repent of their sin and believe in Jesus to enter the kingdom. Historically, gospel missionaries are a leading contributor to the rise of culture and living standards around the world. When people become Christians they typically recognize the value and dignity of every aspect of human life, and so they set about their work as if they were serving the Lord (Col. 3:23–24). This inevitably leads them to produce the highest forms of art, and because they know the joy of being forgiven, even throw really great parties.

2. Willful sin solved by free choice

But education won't solve all of our problems. Sometimes we know what is right and we still choose to do bad things. *Love Wins* talks a lot about sin, and the sins it mentions are typically those social sins we commit against others and the earth. Bell rightly speaks out against greed, injustice, pride, exploitation, racism, molestation, infidelity, rape, genocide, and pollution. But he should also emphasize that all sin is primarily against God. As Cornelius Plantinga Jr. explains in *Not the Way It's Supposed to Be: A Breviary of Sin*,

> Sin is folly...Sin is missing the target...Sin is wandering from the path or rebelling against someone too strong for us or neglecting a good inheritance. Above all, at its core, sin is offense against God.
>
> Why is it not only wrong but also foolish to offend God? God is our final good, our maker and savior, the one in whom alone our restless hearts come to rest. (p. 123)

This fundamental point about sin—that it is primarily an offense to God—is missing from *Love Wins*. Bell does say that we need to be "reconciled to God" and that hell is demanding "the right to be our own god" (pp. 115, 117), but he never indicates that God himself is rightly offended and wrathful toward our rebellion. Bell actually conveys the opposite, for he is sure that a finite human could never do enough bad to merit everlasting punishment from God. Bell asks, "Does God punish people for thousands of years with infinite, eternal

Salvation— Redemption is Not a ledger of Accounts.

torment for things they did in their few finite years of life?" "Can God do this, or even allow this, and still claim to be a loving God?" (p. 2; cf. pp. 102, 175).

If our sin is something that God should be able to get over—if it is not an insurmountable obstacle in our relationship with him—then it stands to reason that Bell thinks we can conquer it through sheer will power. At one point he suggests that our sinful choices can form a rut which can harden into an addiction which is difficult to change, but then he seems to lose interest in the problem and moves on to other things (pp. 104–5). Throughout the book he reminds us that "we are free to accept or reject the invitation to new life that God extends to us. Our choice" (p. 176). So we have the power to choose heaven or hell, even after we are in hell.

Bell hypothesizes about those who have died and gone to hell, "Could God say to someone truly humbled, broken, and desperate for reconciliation, 'Sorry, too late'? Many have refused to accept the scenario in which somebody is pounding on the door, apologizing, repenting, and asking God to be let in, only to hear God say through the keyhole: 'Door's locked. Sorry. If you had been here earlier, I could have done something. But now, it's too late'" (p. 108).

Actually, what Bell cannot imagine is the very thing that Jesus warns will happen. Jesus told the parable of the ten virgins, five of whom foolishly fell asleep and missed the wedding banquet. They pounded on the door and cried, "'Open the door for us!' But he replied, 'Truly I tell you, I don't know you'" (Bell minimizes the danger in this story: see pp. 196–97). Likewise, Jesus warned, "Many will say to me on that day, 'Lord, Lord, did we not prophesy in your name, and in your name drive out demons and in your name perform many miracles?'

Then I will tell them plainly, 'I never knew you. Away from me, you evildoers!'" (Matt. 25:1–13; 7:21–23).

3. Insufficient grace

Bell's Pelagian understanding of our problem and its solution leaves little need for grace. For all its talk about the power of God's love, *Love Wins* is surprisingly graceless. This book rarely mentions the term "grace," and when it does, it's never explained in an Augustinian sense. *Love Wins* uses "grace" as follows: three times in the biblical text being quoted (pp. 126, 134, 189); once in relation to a text from Isaiah that doesn't use the specific word (p. 39); four times to show how conservatives misinterpret it (pp. 11, 27, 64, 97); three times to refer to God's general, common grace (pp. 142, 156, 159); four times to say that God's grace can be rejected (pp. 72, 117 [twice], 176); and once to remind us to extend grace to others (p. 111). Only twice does *Love Wins* mention grace in a way that could be construed as Augustinian—to indicate that the grace extended to the Prodigal Son by his father is generous (p. 168), and to assert that grace is "waiting to pick us up off the ground after we have fallen" (p. 197). However, both of these uses of the word are so vague that they could also be said by a Pelagian.

Bell suggests that "the love of God will melt every hard heart," but he never says how (p. 107). He quotes the prophets who say that

God crushes, refines, tests, corrects, chastens,

A sinner should be living but the Shebat constantly Really he was a slave to sin but God delivered him by his mighty hand and an outstretched arme

None of this conversation suggest conversion is a radical event in the believer's life initiated, conducted & sustained

Sin

and rebukes. (pp. 85–86)

He declares that "Jesus calls disciples in order to *teach* us how to be and what to be" (p. 51; italics added), and that the point of God's judgment is "to *teach* the people, to correct them, to produce something new in them" (p. 85). But these divine actions are all external; they remain outside of the person being corrected. The Augustinian notion that depraved sinners must be reborn by an internal work of the Holy Spirit is entirely missing from *Love Wins* (cf. John 3:3–8; Eph. 2:1–5; Titus 3:4–7).

Bell seems to believe that God's love never stops pursuing us, but that such love is limited in what it can do. God's love can create "potentials" and "possibilities," but it can't change us from the inside out and compel us to love him (p. 116). God can warn us about the dangers of not accepting his acceptance of us, but at the end of the day it's up to us to save ourselves, which we do when we embrace the fact that we are already saved. As confusing as that sounds, it fits Bell's purgatorial understanding of heaven, which, as we saw in chapter three, implies that we are saved by our own efforts as we progressively learn "how to be human all over again" (p. 50). And, as we'll see in the next chapter, it follows logically from his apparent existentialist perspective.

Conclusion

The theology of *Love Wins* appears to be textbook Pelagianism. Like Pelagius, Bell overestimates human beings' natural goodness and underestimates the effects of sin. He believes that we may suffer from ignorance and selfishness, but our wills nevertheless remain strong and healthy enough to choose

God whenever we want, whether in this life or the next. He never mentions that we might need special, redemptive grace, either to choose what is right or to be saved. Apparently we can choose God on our own, using only the natural powers he gave us. The fall has not so deeply corrupted human hearts that people are incapable of straightening out their desires on their own.

If Bell believes that everyone begins life in the family of God and possesses the natural ability to remain there, then it seems that Augustine's penetrating question is particularly relevant. If we don't need the cross to be saved, then "Has Jesus died in vain?" I will examine this question next.

Cross and Resurrection

7

I magine that you and your fiancé together owe $400,000 in school loans. Your future father-in-law sits you both down and says, "I hate to see you start your new life together with such a large financial burden. It might limit your options of where you can live and what jobs you can accept, so my wife and I would like to give you a special wedding gift. We will take care of this debt for you so you can start your marriage with a clean slate. All we ask in return is that you start a charity—perhaps something that I could run on your behalf in my retirement—and that you fund it as you are able."

You gladly hand over your student loan papers, and since you and your spouse are both resident surgeons, you start your new charity with $10,000 of seed money. You realize that your father-in-law's kindness has advanced your financial situation far beyond that of your peers, who will be struggling to make loan payments for years to come. You decide that you are not going to waste your good fortune, so you work hard, save much, and gratefully sink thousands of dollars into your budding charity. You barely notice when decades later your investment reaches half a million dollars. Sure, that is more than your father-in-law originally paid off, but you are a multi-millionaire by now, so you don't need the money and it's doing a lot of good in the world. You enjoy the life you have created for yourself, and your family could not be happier.

That's what makes your discovery so strange. Years later, when your father-in-law dies, you collect the paperwork for the charity that he had been operating. You smile as you read the entries from years gone by—thousands donated for clean water in the Sudan, a scholarship at your alma mater, and dental care for urban youth. But your eyes open wide when you leaf to the first fifteen years of the charity. Every dollar that you and your spouse had donated in those early years—$400,000 plus interest—had been paid to the bank which had serviced your student loans. You let out a scream. Your father-in-law had not paid off your debt at all, but had merely inspired you to do it!

You're not sure whether to laugh or break something. On the one hand his scheme had worked. You are financially secure, you've had a great life, and you've done a lot of good in the world. You admit that you probably wouldn't have been as industrious, especially in the early years, if you had known that much of your income was going to the bank. So in one sense his ruse contributed to your present net worth. On the other hand, you feel cheated. Your father-in-law wasn't as generous as he let on. He didn't sacrifice anything to help you get ahead, but instead used your kindness to give him something to do in retirement.

No analogy is perfect, but the point of this story is that when the need is great, love isn't love unless it actually does something. Sometimes loving parents hold back, patiently giving their children space so they can struggle and figure it out on their own. But if the child truly needs their help, a loving parent steps in and rescues them. Your father-in-law's "gift" may have inspired you to do a lot of good, more than you ever dreamed possible, but you still wouldn't say that he loved you. In the same way, Jesus' death on the cross is an act of love only if it actually accomplishes something. It's not enough to say that it inspires *us* to do something. Because our need is insurmountably huge, it's love only if *he* is actually doing something *for us*. Does the cross change our lives for the better, or does it only inspire us to do so? *W/o faith it is impossible to please God.*

Existentialism

This is the question that came to mind as I read chapter five of *Love Wins*. The church has historically said that Jesus defeated sin, death, and Satan when he bore the penalty of our sin in our place and then rose from the dead. As the apostle John put it, God "sent his Son as an atoning sacrifice for our sins" so that he might "destroy the devil's work" (1 John 4:10; 3:8). John added that Jesus' substitutionary sacrifice also inspires us to follow his example, for "since God so loved us, we also ought to love one another" (1 John 4:11). But of course, this inspiration works only if the cross actually atones for our sins and defeats both death and the devil. The cross isn't love if it doesn't actually save us; so try as we might, it would be difficult to be inspired by it.

Given the importance of "atoning sacrifice" in the biblical understanding of the cross, it is misleading for *Love Wins* to downplay the "sacrificial metaphor" as merely one possible way to understand what happened there. Worse, Bell seems

✳ to believe that we need to move beyond this metaphor, for it doesn't resonate in our culture anymore. He writes that the first Christians used it only because they were surrounded by pagan people who continually offered sacrifices to win the favor of their gods. They described the cross in terms of sacrifice because they wanted to communicate to their Gentile neighbors that "Jesus was the ultimate sacrifice that thoroughly pleased the only God who ever mattered" (p. 125). But, according to Bell, since modern people don't kill animals to appease the gods—and we don't know anyone else who does either—we should move on to fresher, more contemporary models of the cross that speak to us.

Bell's model of choice appears to be existentialism. As the name implies, existentialists wrestle with the problem of existence. They ponder the deep questions of life. Why are we here? What is the meaning of life? Will we live forever, or will death end our existence? Does death make life absurd, or can we trust the universe to take care of us? As Bell asked on one of his speaking tours, "Are the gods angry?"

These are important questions, as far as they go. But the Bible declares that the existentialist's greatest fear—death—is the direct result of sin (Gen. 2:17; Rom. 5:12). So the perennially nagging questions of existence will be taken away only when God solves our problem of sin. Existentialism is on the right track, but it needs to go deeper.

Existentialists desperately want to know, as Bell puts it, that "the universe is on our side" (p. 137). They urgently search for a reason to hang on, to latch onto hope amid the worsening stories of war, genocide, and the destruction of earth. It's no accident that existentialism was popular during and after the

Second World War, and now is making a comeback in our turbulent times.

Christian existentialists find reason for optimism in the death and resurrection of Jesus. For instance, H. Richard Niebuhr, whose career preceded and followed World War II, observed that Jesus' crucifixion is the greatest picture of despair. If ever a life seemed hopelessly lost, it was his. Jesus had done everything right—he had perfectly obeyed his Father—and now he was being crucified for it. Jesus didn't understand, and he cried out in bewildered agony, "My God, my God, why have you forsaken me?" (Matt. 27:46). But in his darkest hour, when it seemed that "being itself" (Niebuhr's name for God) was against him, Jesus somehow managed to keep the faith (Niebuhr 1970, p. 32). He could not comprehend what was going on, yet he firmly spoke into the dark, "Father, into your hands I commit my spirit" (Luke 23:46).

Niebuhr explained that Jesus' faith was rewarded when God raised him from the dead. The resurrection proves that "being itself" can be trusted, that the world really is our friend. We who follow Jesus should be inspired by his example of sacrificial love. We may voluntarily join others in their desperate, God-forsaken predicaments, knowing that the same God who raised Jesus will also raise us from the dead. Regardless of the suffering we endure in this life—regardless of the cross we are called to bear—we may confidently trust that "the universe is on our side." ?universe?

Existentialism in *Love Wins*

Like Niebuhr, Bell writes that Christ's death and resurrection don't accomplish anything new, but merely teach us a general truth about the world. It is the truth that "is built into the very fabric of creation" (p. 131) and is "as old as the universe—that life comes through death" (p. 137). Bell claims that "resurrection after death was not a new idea" for Jesus' disciples, for nature itself taught them that life only comes through death. Bell explains, "For there to be spring, there has to be a fall and then a winter. For nature to spring to life, it first has to die. Death, then resurrection. This is true for ecosystems, food chains, the seasons—it's true all across the environment. Death gives way to life" (p. 130).

Bell suggests that this cosmic truth that life comes through death can also be learned from the act of eating. Plants and animals have to die so we can eat and fuel our lives with them—"The death of one living thing for the life of another." Heroic firefighters illustrate the same universal truth when they sacrifice their lives to rescue others and inspire us to do the same. Bell concludes, "So when the writers of the Bible talk about Jesus's resurrection bringing new life to the world, they aren't talking about a new concept. They're talking about something that has always been true. *It's how the world works.*" The cross is not merely a religious symbol, but points to a deeper, more

> elemental reality, one we all experience every time we take a bite of food.
> Once again, death and rebirth are as old as the world. (pp. 131–32; italics added)

It's important for a Christian existentialist to say that the cross and resurrection aren't accomplishing or even revealing anything new, for the overriding concern of existentialist pastors and theologians is to know that "the universe is on our side." If the cross and resurrection make a radical break with creation—if they do or reveal anything that wasn't already present in the world—then they are an anomaly. Like a black swan, they do not tell us anything about how the world generally is. If Jesus' death and resurrection did something new, they cannot tell us what existentialists desperately need to know—that being is good, the world can be trusted, and "the universe is on our side." Bell does say that the resurrection establishes "a new day" and "a new creation," but he also indicates that this newness is wholly contained within the "huge story" that "John is telling" (pp. 133–34). Something new happened within the biblical story when Jesus rose from the dead, but the story as a whole reveals a general truth which is "as old as the world" (p. 132).

So existentialists view Jesus as a symbol which reveals a general truth about the world. They still may contend that Jesus is an authoritative symbol—because he is God—but they assert that Jesus doesn't reveal anything about the world that you and I couldn't also learn from other sources. To understand why, imagine that a coworker asks you if tomorrow is casual Friday. You assure him that it is, and that he is permitted to wear blue jeans to work. Later, when your boss stops in to say hello, your coworker double-checks with him. When the boss tells him that he may dress casually tomorrow, you turn to him and say, "See, I told you." He replies, "I believed you, but I wanted to hear it from the top." Similarly, existentialists don't believe that Jesus' death and resurrection tell us anything new, but believe instead, as Bell says, that those events authoritatively remind us of the universal truth that "is built into the very fabric of creation" (p. 131).

Christel Alone

This view of Jesus—that he is the authoritative symbol of the truth of the world—enables us to understand Bell's claim that the church's sacraments are merely the way Christians "orient themselves around this mystery" (p. 156) that life comes through death:

> When we baptize,
>
> . . . .
>
> the water signifies death;
> being raised up out of it signifies life.
>
> . . . .
>
> When we take the Eucharist, or Communion,
> we dip bread into a cup,
> enacting and remembering Jesus's gift of himself.
> His body,
> his blood,
> for the life of the world.
> *Our bodies, our lives,*
> *for the life of the world.*
>
> These rituals are true for us,
> because they're true for everybody.
> They unite us, because they unite everybody.
>
> These are signs, glimpses, and tastes of what is true
> for all people in all places at all times—we simply name
> the mystery present in all the world, the gospel already
> announced to every creature under heaven. (p. 157; italics
> added)

Bell's description of the Eucharist seamlessly shifts from Jesus' body to *our* bodies "for the life of the world." Does he mean to say that the Lord's Supper commemorates our sacrifice, and that it has as much significance as Jesus' sacrifice? This makes sense in an existentialist context, for existentialists want to find a general truth about reality. Jesus is not uniquely special, but is merely the authoritative symbol who reveals this general truth. His death and resurrection inform us that life comes from death, but this truth is also revealed by heroic firefighters, winter into spring, seeds that sprout, and the act of chewing. Jesus merely reveals in a big way what alert, thoughtful people should have known all along.

[handwritten note: This minimizes the Cross and puts us on equal par to Christ. Sounds like Satan in Gen 3.]

The Cross

I began this chapter by saying that the cross and resurrection must accomplish something on our behalf to be considered an act of love. Bell's apparently existentialist perspective declares that they do not really accomplish anything—they merely reveal a general truth about creation that we could have learned from other sources. Because for him the cross and resurrection only *reveal* rather than *accomplish*, Bell concludes that they are nothing more than an example for us to follow, the assurance that everything will work out in the end: "When we say yes to God, when we open ourselves to Jesus's living, giving act on the cross, we enter in to a way of life. He is the source, the strength, the *example*, and the *assurance* that this pattern of death and rebirth is the way into the only kind of life that actually sustains and inspires" (p. 136; italics added).

Bell rightly says that the cross is our example, for as the apostle Peter reminds us, "Christ suffered for you, leaving you an example, that you should follow in his steps" (1 Peter 2:21).

But the cross is an inspiring example of love only if it actually accomplishes something in its own right. To use Bell's example of the courageous firefighters on 9/11, their sacrifice is a heroic act of love only because they were actually trying to rescue victims. If I race into a burning building to save a child's life, people will praise me for my selfless love for others. But if the child is standing in a warm blanket beside me, it would be foolish for me to say, "Look how much I love you!" and run into the flames. Likewise, the cross is the greatest act of foolishness—not the greatest act of love—unless it actually rescues us. No rescue, no love. No love, no example. Peter himself makes this point, for soon after he commands us to follow Jesus' example of patient suffering on the cross, Peter explains why: "'He himself bore our sins' in his body on the cross, so that we might die to sins and live for righteousness; 'by his wounds you have been healed'" (1 Peter 2:24).

Because, in Bell's view of the cross in *Love Wins*, the cross merely *reassures* rather than *rescues*, it is ultimately unnecessary. Would our God have endured the cross if it wasn't entirely necessary? Jesus begged his Father in Gethsemane to find, if it was at all possible, another way. If the cross is merely educational, if its sole purpose is to authoritatively inform us that we can trust that "the universe is on our side," then why didn't the Father say, "You know, come to think of it, we could get the word out through a special class or seminar. Perhaps I could write a message in the sky. Or I could use my outdoor voice and thunder, 'Look, people. The truth you need to know is present every spring, every time a plant sends its shoots up through the soil, every time you sit down for breakfast. To him who has ears to hear, I tell you that death is the pathway to life.'" This may sound facetious, but these are Bell's own examples.

It's his idea that the cross is "a symbol of an elemental reality, one we all experience every time we take a bite of food" (p. 131).

Besides making the cross unnecessary, Bell's apparent existentialism also intrudes into his interpretation of the biblical text. He quotes Hebrews 9:26, which says that Jesus "has appeared once for all at the culmination of the ages to do away with sin by the sacrifice of himself" (p. 123). But rather than read this statement as a declaration that Jesus has put an end to the specific yet incomplete sacrifices of the *Hebrews*, Bell interprets this as a general statement about how Jesus' sacrifice put an end to the existential angst of the *Gentiles*. He explains that ancient people worried that the gods might be angry, so they established "whole cultures centered around keeping the gods pleased" (p. 124). They "regularly sacrificed animals—bulls, goats, sheep, birds" (p. 123)—because

> you wanted whoever controlled the sun and rain to be on your side.
> You wanted whoever dictated whether a woman got pregnant to show you favor.
> You wanted the one who decides who wins or loses in battle to decide that you should be victorious. (p. 124)

The point of Hebrews 9:26, writes Bell, is that Jesus' death on the cross has ended the psychological burden of gaining the gods' favor. Now there need be "no more anxiety, no more worry, no more stress, no more wondering if the gods were pleased with you or ready to strike you down. There was no more need for any of that sacrifice, because Jesus was the ultimate sacrifice that thoroughly pleased the only God who ever mattered" (p. 125).

The main problem with this interpretation is that the verse in question appears in a book entitled Hebrews, which had Jewish rather than Gentile offerings in mind. Hebrews could not have been written to the Gentiles because from the very beginning the loving relationship between God and his people was different from the anxious relationships that pagans had with their supposed gods. Baal, Molech, and Diana were not gracious and compassionate, slow to anger, and tenderly loving. They did not yearn to redeem their people, but insisted on sacrifice to soothe the volatile temperaments. The relationship between God and his people was never based on appeasement, but on God's love and covenantal promise. This love and promise go all the way back to Genesis 12, where Yahweh made his first promise to Abram, who responded faithfully by building two altars to the Lord.

The author of Hebrews explains that the cross fulfills the sacrifices of the Old Testament, particularly those offered on the annual Day of Atonement. The Jews did not sacrifice bulls and goats because they mistakenly thought that the gods were angry. They sacrificed animals because God said this was necessary for him to forgive their sin (Leviticus 16:15–17). The book of Hebrews declares that these offerings pointed to the ultimate sacrifice of Christ, who put an end to Jewish animal sacrifice when he "entered the Most Holy Place once for all by his own blood, thus obtaining eternal redemption" (Heb. 9:12).

So Scripture does not teach that Jesus' death and resurrection supplies peace of mind to pagan people who mistakenly thought that the powers of the world were against them. Instead, it clearly proclaims, both in particular passages and in the complete arc of its narrative, that Jesus' death and resurrection supplies the ground for the forgiveness of sin (which then provides peace of mind). The central question of the Bible is not the existential concern, "Is the universe on my side?" Rather it is the cry of a broken and defeated rebel, "How can a sinner like me and a fallen world like this ever receive the righteousness and peace of a holy God?" The answer you find in Scripture depends a great deal on whether you're asking the correct question.

Conclusion

One problem with an existential perspective on the Christian faith is that it minimizes our need for Jesus. If all we need from the cross is an inspirational example to follow, then we must not be in very serious trouble. Indeed, as I implied in my opening story, if we think that a cross which only inspires is nevertheless an act of love, then we must not think that we need much help. There is a logical connection from the Pelagianism discussed in chapter six to the example-only theory of the atonement examined here.

Another problem with an existential perspective is that it tends to look past the *person* of Jesus to the universal *principle* he represents. Rather than cherish Jesus and find our salvation solely in him, this view says that he came to point us to the general truth that "life comes through death." We are "saved" when we embrace this cosmic truth, and since we can access this truth without even knowing about Jesus, we can potentially be saved apart from hearing the gospel. We are saved by discovering a general truth about the world, not by the person and work of Christ.

And so Bell ends chapter five, as he began it, with the story of Eminem's possible conversion. Bell noticed that Eminem wore a cross around his neck during a concert, and he wondered, "Did he stumble into that truth that's as old as the universe—that life comes through death?" Had he learned that "the universe is on our side"? Bell concludes that this existential truth is the reason "the cross continues to endure. It's a reminder, a sign, a glimpse, an icon that allows us to tap into our deepest longings to be part of a new creation" (p. 137).

I agree that Jesus fulfills our "deepest longings to be part of a new creation," but we can participate in the new creation only if we believe in Jesus—not the principle he represents, but his actual person. Jesus himself declared that "the Son of Man must be lifted up, that everyone who believes in him may have eternal life…Whoever believes in him is not condemned, but whoever does not believe stands condemned already because they have not believed in the name of God's one and only Son" (John 3:14–15 , 18). Jesus, the real person, the very Son of God, completed the sacrifice that pays off all of the debts of those who truly believe in him.

The Christian faith is primarily not about principles or general truths but about a person, Jesus Christ. He is the subject of the next chapter.

Jesus

8

A panda walks into a café. He orders a sandwich, eats it, then pulls out a gun and shoots the waiter. "Why?" groans the injured man. The panda shrugs and plunks a badly punctuated wildlife manual onto the table. "Look me up," he growls and walks out the door. The waiter stumbles to his feet and opens the book to the entry for *panda*. It reads, "Panda: Large, black and white bear-like mammal native to China. Eats, shoots and leaves."

This punch line became the title of a best-selling book (Truss, *Eats, Shoots & Leaves*) on punctuation (yes, you read that right), because it cleverly illustrates the unfortunate consequences of a misplaced comma. In this case the comma separated "eats" and "shoots," turning the latter from a noun into a verb and producing one confused, though apparently literate, panda.

Theologians tell a similar, though less humorous story (you know you're in trouble when grammarians tell better jokes than you!). As legend has it, a theological liberal was trying to make the point to his class that God was nothing more than a larger version of us, so he wrote on the chalkboard, "God is other people." This statement disturbed one of his more conservative students, and after class the student defended God's honor by surreptitiously walking to the board and inserting a comma between "other" and "people." Now the sentence read, "God is other, people." Theologians call the student's insertion the "transcendence comma" because it reminds us of the infinite chasm between God and us.

Both of these stories—one funny and the other told by theologians—illustrate how crucial it is to make necessary distinctions. A trained ear can easily hear the difference between a C and a C-sharp, a master artist knows that the color periwinkle is not the same as lavender, and a finish carpenter can feel the difference between a pine board and a piece of oak. You may not be able to tell the difference between any of these, but aren't you thankful to live in a world full of musicians, painters, and craftsmen who can?

This classic need for distinctions is what is missing from chapter six of *Love Wins*. This chapter runs together so many different things that ultimately it clouds and even changes the meaning of the Christian gospel. It desperately needs a few well-placed theological commas. Specifically, the chapter fails to distinguish between general and redemptive history, Jesus' roles as Creator and Redeemer, common and special grace, and the truth of Christianity and other religions. Collapsing together these important distinctions enables Bell to conclude that every adherent of every religion may be saved, but it also downplays the significance of Jesus Christ.

As we will see, while it's important to make distinctions in every area of life, it's especially essential in theology. Failure to discriminate in the arts may result in an ugly painting or a wrong note, but in theology the consequences can be fatal.

General and Redemptive History

Chapter six of *Love Wins*—"There Are Rocks Everywhere"— was inspired by Bell's reading of 1 Corinthians 10. There the apostle Paul alludes to the Exodus 17 story when God told Moses to strike a rock so that water would gush out and slake the Israelites' thirst. Since the Israelites received nourishment from the rock, Paul concludes that the rock was a type of Christ. He writes that the Israelites all "drank from the spiritual rock that accompanied them, and that rock was Christ" (1 Cor. 10:4).

Bell takes Paul's rather straightforward comment and runs right past the theological comma, extrapolating Paul's statement out about as far as one can. He claims that Paul means we are authorized to find Jesus everywhere, even when no one is aware that he is around:

Jesus was there,
Without anybody using his name.
Without anybody saying that it was him.
Without anybody acknowledging just what—or, more precisely, who—it was.

Paul's interpretation that Christ was present in the Exodus raises the question:
Where else has Christ been present?
When else?
With who else?
How else?

Paul finds Jesus there,
in that rock,
because Paul finds Jesus everywhere" (p. 144).

Paul did find Jesus everywhere, but in a much more nuanced way. Paul was not referring to Jesus' general presence everywhere in world history—though he is there—but to Jesus' anonymous presence in the special, redemptive history of God's people. The rock that Paul references is a very special rock on a very special journey. The Exodus is the paradigmatic redemptive event of the Old Testament, God's unique act of deliverance which prepares the world for all that Jesus came to do. Just as God delivered the people of Israel from their bondage in Egypt, leading them across the wilderness and into the Promised Land, so Jesus came to rescue us from our slavery to sin and death, sending his Spirit to sustain and guide us as we make our way to our Promised Land.

When Paul said that the rock was a symbol that pointed to Christ, he meant that just as Jesus saves his people now, so he was the one who was saving his people in the Old Testament. Jesus himself made the connection, telling Jews who identified with the Exodus story, "Let anyone who is thirsty come to me and drink. Whoever believes in me, as Scripture has said, rivers of living water will flow from within them" (John 7:37–38).

Here's the point: Paul wasn't saying that we should look for Jesus in or behind every rock in the world. He wasn't referring to God's omnipresent and providential care for his creation, though we thank God that he lovingly supplies the needs of every living thing (Ps. 104:27–30). Paul was simply explaining to the Corinthian church that they belonged to the same spiritual family as God's people in the Old Testament. And they should be careful, for if Jews who had been saved by Christ were able to fall into idolatry, then the Corinthians should watch lest the same fate happen to them (1 Cor. 10:5–13).

Jesus as Creator and Redeemer

In addition to collapsing redemptive into general history, *Love Wins* doesn't clearly distinguish between Jesus' roles as Creator and Redeemer. Bell understands that distinctions are important to properly talk about Jesus, for he writes, "When people use the word 'Jesus,' then, it's important for us to ask who they're talking about" (p. 156). Bell rightly rejects nationalistic and imperialistic images of Jesus that some might use to sanctify their own "greed and lust for power" (p. 156), but he doesn't seem to appreciate the distinction between Jesus' work as Creator and as Redeemer.

The apostle Paul declares that Jesus the Creator is the omnipresent ruler of the universe. He "fills everything in every way" (Eph. 1:23), and "in him all things hold together" (Col. 1:17). But Jesus performs his role as Redeemer by doing a specific work in a specific place. Jesus didn't redeem us by sovereignly filling "everything in every way" but by dying on the cross for our sins and rising again (Rom. 4:25). He then sent his Spirit to regenerate and empower everyone who repents of their sin and believes on his name (Titus 3:3–8). Now Jesus intercedes for us before the Father in heaven (Heb. 4:14–16), indwells us by his Spirit (1 Cor. 6:19), and leads us as head of the church (Col. 1:18).

Gospel

Thus, Jesus' work as Creator and his work as Redeemer are two related but clearly distinct roles. Jesus' act of creating and governing the world is not the same as his act of redeeming it. They differ in meaning, method, and timing. They are as different as home repair (redemption) is from new construction (creation), as a mechanic shop differs from a new car lot, or as emergency surgery differs from childbirth.

It's surprising, then, to read in *Love Wins* that Jesus' presence as Creator is redemptive, or—to say it from the other direction—that Jesus redeems the world by his presence in creation. Bell declares that Jesus is right now saving "everybody, every nation, every ethnic group, every tribe" (p. 149), and he is doing this by holding "the entire universe in his embrace" (p. 157). Bell suggests that Jesus is

> a force, an energy, a being calling out to us
> . . . .
> trying to get our attention. (p. 141)

Jesus is

> the love that creeps in, with no explanation, at the strangest times,
> the quiet grace that grabs hold of us in the middle of the night and assures us that we're going to be fine. (p. 142)

He is the "energy, spark, and electricity that pulses through all of creation" and that "sustains it, fuels it, and keeps it going. Growing, evolving, reproducing, making more" (p. 145).

Besides using a somewhat mystical description of Jesus' role as Creator (is he a "force," "energy," or "spark"?), *Love Wins* mistakenly assumes that Jesus "saves" people merely by sustaining and preserving their lives. Bell asserts that Jesus is "the very life source of the universe who has walked among us and continues to sustain everything with his love and power and grace and energy" (p. 156). It is this sustaining and preserving love which is "the gospel already announced to every creature under heaven" (p. 157). Whenever anyone stumbles upon the idea that they are loved, that some force or energy is holding the universe together, then they are having "an honest, authentic encounter with the living Christ. He is the rock, and there is water for the thirsty there, wherever *there* is" (p. 158). And so people are "redeemed" by Jesus' act of caring for creation:

> Not everybody sees it,
> not everybody recognizes it,
> but everybody is sustained by it. (p. 161)

This confusion between Jesus' roles as Creator and Redeemer often arises in Christian existentialism. As I mentioned in the last chapter, Bell's book seems to make the case that our central problem is that we aren't sure that the universe is our friend. According to the *Grand Rapids Press* (April 4, 2011, p. A2), Bell said in a local talk promoting *Love Wins* that "the cross resonates with our culture because we desperately want to know that we're not alone." If the main point of the cross, which is the climax of redemption, is to inform us of the creational truth that "we're not alone," then it makes sense that *Love Wins* would conflate Jesus' creation and redemption. In *Love Wins*, both of Jesus' important roles are essentially performing the same work, for redemption merely affirms the general creational truth that God made and loves us. But of course, if redemption does the same work as creation, then ultimately redemption is unnecessary.

Common and Special Grace

Bell's intermingling of creation and redemption also erases the essential distinction between common and special grace. Common grace includes the innumerable nonsalvific gifts that God showers upon creation. He provides us with sound bodies and minds, surrounds us with good friends, supplies us with paying jobs, sends sunshine and rain to grow our crops, enables artists, scientists, and technicians to create new products that bring joy to life, restrains our sinful impulses so no one behaves as badly as they might, and even motivates us all to sacrifice a little—and sometimes a lot—for the benefit of someone we barely know. In these ways and more, common grace not only preserves our lives but also makes them worth living.

We thank God for common grace, and couldn't imagine living in a world without it. We seriously couldn't imagine it, for without common grace you couldn't read that last sentence, and I wouldn't have been able to write it. But as indispensable as common grace indisputably is, God's "common" (or "general") gifts of creation have never saved anyone. Common grace is like the long reliever in baseball. This is the pitcher who enters the game in the third inning, after his team has fallen behind by five or so runs. His job is not to win the game, but to keep the other team from scoring so that his team has a chance to catch up. Likewise, common grace doesn't redeem creation, but it keeps us in the game. Common grace sustains creation long enough so Jesus can come and save us.

Jesus the Creator blesses the world with common grace, but as Redeemer he comes with special, saving grace. Jesus spoke of his unique, redemptive role when he announced to the world, "I am the way and the truth and the life. No one comes to the Father except through me" (John 14:6). Remark-ably, Bell interprets this verse merely as another expression of common grace. He writes that Jesus doesn't tell us "how, or when, or in what manner the mechanism functions that gets people to God through him. He doesn't even state that those coming to the Father through him will even know that they are coming exclusively through him. He simply claims that whatever God is doing in the world to know and redeem and love and restore the world is happening through him" (p. 154).

In *Love Wins*, the point of John 14:6 is that "the all-embracing, saving love of this particular Jesus the Christ will of course include all sorts of unexpected people from across the cultural spectrum." It will include "Muslims, Hindus, Buddhists, and Baptists from Cleveland." Bell declares that Jesus "is saving everybody" by the simple fact that as Creator, he is "as wide as the universe...containing every single particle of creation" (p. 155).

Bell is mistaken about John 14:6, however, for the context of this passage clearly indicates that the "mechanism...that gets people to God through him" is belief in Jesus. John 14 repeatedly exhorts readers to believe in Jesus. Jesus tells his disciples to *believe* in him (14:1), to know the Father through *knowing* him (14:7, 9), and again to *believe* in him (14:12). Indeed, the point of John's gospel is that "you may *believe* that Jesus is the Christ, the Son of God, and that by believing you may have life in his name" (20:31; italics added). This is why John continually tells stories that remind his readers to believe in Jesus. His gospel records Jesus saying, "Whoever *believes* in [God's one and only son] shall not perish but have eternal life" (3:16); "whoever *believes* in me will never be thirsty" (6:35); "the one who *believes* in me will live, even though he dies" (11:25); and "no one who *believes* in me [shall] stay in darkness" (12:46).

In addition to these clear statements that belief in Jesus is *the* necessary "mechanism that gets people to God," John also unequivocally warns of the judgment that awaits those who don't believe. Bell quotes John 12:47, which states that Jesus did not come "to judge the world" (p. 160), but he omits the very next verse, which declares that "there is a judge for the one who rejects me and does not accept my words" (12:48). These words include Jesus' warning that "whoever *believes* in [God's Son] is not condemned, but whoever does *not believe* stands *condemned* already because they have not believed in the name of God's one and only Son" (3:18). And to make the point undeniably clear, John adds, "Whoever *believes* in the Son has eternal life, but whoever *rejects* the Son will *not see life*, for *God's wrath remains on them* (3:36; italics added).

The apostle John wrote his gospel so that we might put our faith in the special, redemptive grace of Jesus (20:31). Common grace is wonderful, but no one has ever been saved by their warm feelings about the universe on a bluebird day in May. If our only problem is existential angst, then perhaps learning that life is good would be enough. But if our problem is the deeper issue of sin, we're going to need the special grace of the cross.

Christianity and Other Religions

The payoff from collapsing redemptive into general history, redemption into creation, and special into common grace is that it enables *Love Wins* to assume a potentially less offensive posture toward other world religions. Because in the book Jesus is merely the symbol of the general goodness we find in the world, Bell logically concludes that "Jesus is bigger than any one religion…He will always transcend whatever cages and labels are created to contain and name him, especially the one called 'Christianity'" (p. 150). He adds,

> Jesus is supracultural.
> He is present within all cultures,
> and yet outside of all cultures.
>
> He is for all people,
> and yet he refuses to be co-opted or owned by any one culture.
>
> That includes any Christian culture…We can point to him, name him, follow him, discuss him, honor him, and believe in him—but we cannot claim him to be ours any more than he's anyone else's. (pp. 151–52)

Bell's position seems similar to the view held by Karl Rahner (1904–1984), who claimed that anyone in any religion (or not) who opened themselves to the grace that is present in nature could be considered an "anonymous Christian" (p. 218). They would be "saved" by the natural or common grace offered by Christ, even if they were unaware that it was him. Likewise, Bell writes that while Jesus declares that "he, and he alone, is saving everybody," his salvation is "way, way open," as "wide as the universe," so that it takes in anyone who is open to "the mystery present in all the world" (pp. 155, 157).

Bell writes that these anonymous Christians may not "use the exact language we use" (p. 158), for

> sometimes people use his name;
> other times they don't.

> Some people have so much baggage with regard to the
> name "Jesus" that when they encounter the mystery present
> in all of creation—grace, peace, love, acceptance, healing,
> forgiveness—the last thing they are inclined to name it is
> "Jesus." (p. 159)

Regardless of what they call it, says Bell, the common grace
that non-Christians are responding to is Jesus. And since
Jesus is everywhere in creation, he is impossible to avoid. Bell
concludes that Jesus

> is the answer,
> but he is also the question,
> the hunt,
> the search,
> the exploration,
> the discovery.
>
> He is the rock,
> and there is water there. (p. 161)

Anonymous Christians?

What are we to make of the idea that there are "anonymous
Christians," who don't even know Jesus' name, let alone that
he is the Redeemer of the world? First, this concept of anonymous Christianity is a close cousin to religious pluralism. It's
a short step from saying that every religion may contain some
truth about Jesus which leads to God, to saying that every
religion simply leads directly to God. Retaining Jesus as the
middleman may enable us to project a Christian aura around
our religious pluralism, but practically it makes very little

difference. Anonymous Christianity cashes out as *functional pluralism*, for it encourages everyone to pursue the particular "saving" truth that is found in their own religion. Does it really matter if we say this truth is secretly Jesus?

Bell says that he is not a pluralist, for he believes that Jesus "alone is saving everybody" and that it's not true that every religion is an equally acceptable path up the mountain to God (pp. 154–55). Yet *Love Wins* highlights Huston Smith's *The Soul of Christianity* for "further reading" to learn more about "who and what God is" (p. 201). Smith's book unabashedly argues for pluralism, saying that "though for Christians God is *defined* by Jesus, he is not *confined* to Jesus" (p. 16). Smith claims that when Christians say that Jesus is best they are merely speaking as a man might talk about his wife. Smith writes, "When a man says that his wife means the world to him, he is not claiming that she should mean the world to other men." Instead, this man means only that his love for his wife is "absolute and can brook no rivals" (p. 13). Moreover, such a man "*does* believe that all men should feel for their wives the *love* that he feels for his wife. In our multicultural age Christians are coming to understand this point" (p. 14). According to Smith, the world's religions are like wives—it doesn't matter which one you have as long as you love her.

Second, anonymous Christianity is often perceived as yet another imperialistic move by Western Christians. As Stephen Prothero demonstrates in *God Is Not One*, the various religions of the world are more different than they are alike. Other religions certainly don't think that they are merely supplying Muslim or Buddhist perspectives on Jesus. Just as we would be offended to be told that we are "anonymous Hindus" or "anonymous Muslims," so it sounds disrespectful to inform other religions that they are unwittingly embracing our Savior.

My point here is not to discourage evangelism, but simply to say that anonymous Christianity does not avoid charges of imperialism and aggression.

Third, both religious pluralism and anonymous Christianity cheapen the costly sacrifice of Christ. As Augustine wrote in *On Nature and Grace*, if anyone can be saved by embracing the good in nature, then "Christ has died in vain" (Augustine 2011, p. 320). It's well and good for Christians to reach out to those who feel excluded and let them know that they are loved and embraced by God. However, if we tell those on the margins that their religion may possess sufficient grace to save them, then we are essentially pushing Jesus to the margins in order to reach them. We may think that it's *nice* that Jesus died on the cross for us, but we can no longer say why it's *necessary.* If Jesus' death and resurrection are nothing more than a symbol of God's universal love—a sign that everything is good and right with the world—then there really is no need to proclaim the good news that Jesus is the Christ who offers eternal life to those who believe specifically in him.

Finally, it's impossible to square the openness in *Love Wins* to the good in other religions (pp. 158–59) with what we find in Scripture. Bell suggests that Jesus' statement "I have other sheep that are not of this sheep pen" (John 10:16) indicates that Jesus has come to save people who remain in other religions (p. 152). Actually, Jesus is merely telling his Jewish audience that he has come to bring both Jews and Gentiles (the "other sheep") to faith in him.

Scripture never celebrates when people from other religions have what Bell calls divine "encounters" which "profoundly affect them" (p. 158). Instead, God told the Israelites that when they entered the Promised Land they must "break down their [the nations'] altars, smash their sacred stones and burn their Asherah poles in the fire; cut down the idols of their gods and wipe out their names from those places" (Deut. 12:3). When the Israelites stopped smashing idols and instead sought common ground with Baal, God burned their cities and exiled them into captivity (2 Kings 21:3–16; 23:26–27).

God's substantive opposition to other religions continues in the New Testament. When Paul was given a platform on Mars Hill, he used the opportunity to tell his philosophical audience the many ways that their religious practices were wrong. He used the common ground of their Greek poets and statue to the unknown God to inform them that they did not know the true and living God and that they were foolish to suppose that their temples and worship were pleasing to him. Paul declared that "in the past God overlooked such ignorance, but now he commands all people everywhere to repent. For he has set a day when he will judge the world" (Acts 17:30–31).

We who follow Jesus should seek to live at peace with all people, even and especially with those who belong to other religions. We may and should engage in interreligious dialogue which seeks to understand the world from their perspective. But we must never forget that when it comes to the matter of salvation—of saving grace—those of other faiths ultimately need to believe not in the general goodness of the world but in the very Jesus who died and rose again for their sin. The Bible never suggests that there might be anonymous Christians, and neither should we.

Conclusion

Love Wins aims to open the door to salvation as wide as possible. But as I have explained in this chapter, it's impossible to open the floodgates without either ignoring or wrenching from context a large number of salvation-specific biblical texts. Moreover, the church historically has studied such texts and developed important theological distinctions from them. These include crucial distinctions between general and redemptive history, Jesus' roles as Creator and Redeemer, common and special grace, and the truth of Christianity and other religions' truth claims. For some people, these kinds of distinctions might not seem critically important. For evangelicals, however, such nuance is crucially significant in conducting the kinds of theological exploration that Bell seeks to undertake. Language is one of God's common gifts for faithful Christians to use so that we might both know Jesus more intimately and hold ourselves accountable for putting commas in their proper places.

The kinds of biblical and theological issues that I discussed in this chapter related to Jesus are best understood as part of the doctrine of God. So in the next chapter I address this foundational issue: what does the Bible teach about God and how does that square with the God presented in *Love Wins*?

God

9

A man is on trial for a robbery that everyone admits he probably committed. There were eyewitnesses, surveillance tapes, and to make matters worse for him, he was apprehended while in the act of committing the crime. But rather than concede his guilt, the man acts as his own attorney and attempts to turn the tables on the criminal justice system. He informs the court that he has lived a pretty good life, and though he's made mistakes now and again—who hasn't?—he has many friends who will testify that he's a really nice man. He's certainly too nice for jail.

A tremor shudders down the man's body as he turns to face the jury. He jabs his finger into the air and asks, "And what's the deal with prisons? What does it say about us as a society, that we happily lock people up and throw away the key? If we really are the kind and generous people that we claim to be, why don't we rehabilitate those who have lost their way?"

He pauses, steadies himself, then quietly pleads, "Men and women of the jury, most honorable judge, don't harden your hearts and put me away—I still have so much love I want to share with the world. My family needs me. Don't let my little boy grow up without his daddy."

His voice begins to rise as he makes his closing pitch: "Let this be the day that goodness and love triumph in the world! There may be other days when revenge and vindictiveness have their way, but this is not their day! This is the day that you showed the world that you are kindhearted and good people! This is the day that you stood up for forgiveness and mercy, because you know they are the future!"

A shadow crosses the man's face and he begins to cry. "All I'm asking," he begs, "is that you put yourselves in my shoes. To tell you the truth, I don't feel safe in this courtroom. I honestly don't. I'm not sure, honorable judge and esteemed jury, that you are on my side. Are you with me? Please, please, take my side." His voice tapers off as he buries his head in his arms and sobs.

What an awkward, uncomfortable scene! It's so easy to get caught up in the man's emotional appeal that we forget that the only reason we're here is that this man has probably done something very bad. The alleged thief effectively "flipped the script," making it seem as if the judge and jury were on trial rather than him.

Is God on Trial?

I composed this strange story to illustrate what I believe occurs in *Love Wins*. We all are known rebels against God who deserve his punishment, but rather than accept what we have coming, *Love Wins* attempts to make our judgment about God rather than about us. Rob Bell effectively puts God on trial, for he makes the same kind of arguments as the person in my example: (1) we don't deserve our punishment, (2) judgment must be rehabilitative rather than penal, (3) God is unloving if he punishes people forever, and (4) we desperately need to feel safe. I will respond to each of Bell's assertions in the body of this chapter, but before I do, I want to briefly discuss whether we should ask such questions and, if so, how.

First, my story sets the correct context, for a courtroom rather than a family is the right analogy for describing God's relationship to the entire world. Bell uses the story of the prodigal son to argue that every person is in the family of God and has God as their Father. He declares that it doesn't matter who we are or what we've done, because the parable teaches us

> the sure and certain truth that we are loved…
>
> . . . .
>
> God has made peace with us. (p. 172)

Rather than resist God's universal and undying love, we must simply learn to trust our Father when he says, "You are always with me, and everything I have is yours" (p. 172).

The problem with Bell's analogy is that the Bible never says that God is the Father of everyone. In a general, nonredemptive sense, Adam is "the son of God" (Luke 3:38) and "we are God's offspring" (Acts 17:29), but God reserves the title of "Father" for his most intimate relationships. Scripture tells us that God is the Father of Jesus Christ (Heb. 1:1–14), and that through Jesus he is our Father, too (Eph. 1:5). God has adopted us into his family—which implies that we began life outside that family—by the redemptive work of Jesus Christ (Gal. 4:5; Rom. 8:15). Those who do not receive Jesus' redemption remain outside of the family of God. So Jesus told a group of Jews that their father was actually Satan rather than God, for they did not love God's Son (John 8:42–47). And David said that the LORD pours fatherly "compassion on those who fear him," which assumes that God does not act as a father toward those who don't (Ps. 103:13).

Scripture does not say that God is the Father of all, but it does teach that "God is the *King* of all the earth" (Ps. 47:7; cf. Rev. 17:14; 19:16) and that he is the "*Judge* of all the earth" (Gen. 18:25; cf. Ps. 94:2; 96:13). As Paul announced in his sermon on Mars Hill, God "has set a day when he will judge the world with justice by the man he has appointed" (Acts 17:31). If God is everyone's King and Judge, then it's fitting to examine our relationship to him within the context of a courtroom.

Second, it's essential that we remember our place in that courtroom. We are the defendant, the one who is deservedly on trial. It's appropriate and even helpful to ask questions of God, as long as we remember two things: we are the criminal in this scene, so our perspective is bound to be skewed; and we won't have any chance at correction unless we submit our questions and doubts to the authority of God's Word. When we encounter passages of Scripture that are difficult to accept, we should wrestle with and do our best to understand them. But we must never disregard them. In order to conduct an honest, constructive dialogue about God and salvation, we must account for every passage of Scripture, especially the hard ones.

Third, we must not substitute emotional appeals for the clear teaching of Scripture. *Love Wins* asks those of us who are evangelicals to own up to what our understanding of hell implies about God. If we believe that someone must repent of their sins and believe in Jesus to be saved, then how many people do we realistically expect will end up in hell? Millions?

Billions? Most of communist North Korea, Muslim Afghanistan, and Hindu India? If so many people are sent to hell forever, how can we plausibly say that God is good?

We evangelicals respond that we don't know how many people will go to hell. Such decisions belong to God, not to us. However, since Jesus said the way is broad which leads to destruction (Matt. 7:13), and since many have probably died without believing in Jesus, the number may be high. But rather than become crushed by this dismal news, evangelicals historically have used the imminent danger of hell as a motivation for gospel missions. The great missionary movements of the nineteenth and twentieth centuries arose from the evangelical belief that lost people need the Lord. This *is* an emotional issue for us because of our love for Jesus and our desire to share his good news of eternal life with others.

We evangelicals also say that while the kind of argument in *Love Wins* is emotionally powerful, the question about hell is too important to be settled on the basis of subjective feelings. Ultimately it doesn't matter how we or anyone else *feels* about hell, but only what God says about it. So rather than cram the biblical view of God into our finite, human boxes, saying that "if there was an earthly father who was like that, we would call the authorities" (p. 174), we should take our cues from God's Word. If Scripture declares that God punishes people in hell forever, then who are we to say that he is unloving and unjust to do so? If we believe the Bible is the Word of God, wouldn't it make more sense for us to say that we must be missing something?

So we will wrestle with the questions raised in *Love Wins*, for if we're honest, we must admit that we've all wondered about them. But we should also admit, right off the top, that there is something strange about this project, and if we're not careful, it can become downright perverse. At the end of the day, we are the ones on trial, not God.

Do We Deserve Eternal Punishment?

Love Wins declares that we are sinners, but it also repeatedly asserts that everlasting torment in hell is far more punishment than anyone deserves. It begins with the rhetorical question, "Does God punish people for thousands of years with infinite, eternal torment for things they did in their few finite years of life?" (p. 2). In the middle it asks, "Have billions of people been created only to spend eternity in conscious punishment and torment, suffering infinitely for the finite sins they committed in the few years they spent on earth?" (p. 102). And near the end Bell declares,

> If something is wrong with your God
>
> . . . .
>
> if your God will punish people for all of eternity for sins committed in a few short years,
> no amount of clever marketing
>
> . . . .
>
> will be able to disguise
> that one, true, glaring, untenable, unacceptable, awful reality. (p. 175)

This seemingly reasonable argument—that a finite person could never merit unending punishment—overlooks the important fact that culpability is determined largely by the identity of the victim. You barely notice when a person inadvertently steps on an ant or swats a fly. But if that person just for kicks decides to pull the legs off a frog, you sit up and pay attention. If they cut the tails off squirrels, you start to worry; and if they begin to torture puppies, you're going to turn them in to the authorities. If they graduate to killing another human being, they're going to jail and maybe to the electric chair. And if this person seeks to destroy the infinite and holy God, what then would they deserve?

We may not have literally killed God, but that is only from lack of opportunity. We all were born with the insatiable desire to eliminate God so that we can take his place. If we're honest, we sadly hear our own voices in the crowd chanting, "Crucify him! Crucify him!" (Luke 23:21). And what does such arrogant ingratitude deserve?

Anselm tells us this in his eleventh-century classic, *Why God Became Man*. In this dialogue with his friend Boso, Anselm demonstrates the gravity of sin. He asks Boso whether it would be permissible even to cast a glance in the direction in which God said not to look. When Boso says no, Anselm asks whether it would be permissible to look where God said not to look, even if doing so would save the entire world from perishing. Boso replies that although "it is a lightweight matter…I have no alternative but to admit that, for the sake of preserving the whole of creation, there is nothing which I ought to do contrary to the will of God." What if doing so would save an infinite number of worlds? Anselm asks. Even so, replies Boso. Anselm concludes, "This is how seriously we sin, whenever we knowingly do anything, however small, contrary to the will of God. For we are always in his sight, and it's always the teaching he gives us that we should not sin" (Anselm, p. 306).

If Anselm's view seems overly harsh, it may be because we have lost our wonder at the glorious majesty of God. Why are we troubled by the existence of hell, but not so much by what happened on the cross? Shouldn't the unimaginable suffering of the innocent Son of God bother us even more than the awful torment of hell? Furthermore, doesn't the existence of the cross indicate that we actually deserve hell?

Look at this from God's perspective. If desperate situations call for extreme measures, then extreme measures are a sign we are in a desperate situation. When a police car flashes its lights behind me, my wife may say in her disapproving voice, "What did you do?" If my car is surrounded by police and a television helicopter is hovering overhead, my wife's tone becomes more accusatory: "*What* did you *do?*" If a fighter jet joins the chase, dropping bombs toward our car, my wife may scream like the leading lady in a Schwarzenegger movie, "*What did you do?!*"

Consider what God did to save us. He didn't hand us a brochure, as if our problem was merely ignorance. He didn't call a meeting, as if our problem was merely stubbornness. He answered our need with the cross, which can only mean we have royally messed up. If the cross is necessary to save us, then *What did we do?* *good*

We have rebelled against God, causing both his death and ours. So as hard as this is to accept, of course we deserve hell. Anything less would be a grave injustice.

Must Judgment Be Rehabilitative?

The answer to this question is already implied in the previous answer, but it's worth noting that Bell believes that a loving God will not punish people simply because they deserve it but will always punish with a view toward their improvement. He observes that the Old Testament prophets said that

God crushes,

refines,

tests,

corrects,

chastens,

and rebukes—

but always with a purpose.

No matter how painful, brutal, oppressive, no matter how far people find themselves from home because of their sin, indifference, and rejection, there's always the assurance that it won't be this way *forever*. (pp. 85–86; italics original)

Bell suggests that hell is nothing more than the natural consequences for bad choices. People create their own hells when they reject "God's very essence, which is love." God allows them to choose hell if they want, but he never uses hell as his punishment for their sin (pp. 176–77).

While it's true that hell is the natural consequence for human rebellion, this doesn't go far enough. The apostle Paul clearly states that hell is God's punishment on sinners: "Because of your stubbornness and your unrepentant heart, you are storing up wrath against yourself for the day of God's wrath, when his righteous judgment will be revealed" (Rom. 2:5). And Jesus will return to "punish those who do not know God and do not obey the gospel of our Lord Jesus. They will be punished with everlasting destruction" (2 Thess. 1:8–9).

If hell is not a penalty, then it's difficult to explain why Jesus died. If hell is merely the natural consequences of our sinful choices, then how does the cross prevent us from going there?

Without the penal nature of hell, it's impossible to explain how Jesus bore our curse in our place (Gal. 3:13). If we say that hell is not a penalty, it won't be long until we lose the cross.

Is God Unloving If He Punishes Forever?

This question appears to be the main reason why Bell wrote *Love Wins*. He explains from the start that he intends to overthrow the idea that God will save only a few select people and send everyone else to hell. "Can God do this," Bell asks, "or even allow this, and still claim to be a loving God?" (p. 2). Later he answers his own question, stating that a God who says he loves you and then throws you into hell the moment you die is

> …simply devastating.
> Psychologically crushing.
> We can't bear it.
> No one can.
>
> And that is the secret deep in the heart of many people, especially Christians: they don't love God. They can't, because the God they've been presented with and taught about can't be loved. That God is terrifying and traumatizing and unbearable. (pp. 174–75)

What can we say to this question? Is God unloving if he punishes people forever? I have four responses, each one building on the one before.

1. God's love requires God to be holy, and God's holiness requires the infinite punishment of our sin.

Expressed differently, God isn't loving if he isn't holy (see chapter one, under "Is Your God Too Small?"), and he isn't holy if he does not punish our sin with infinite wrath. Thus, by the transitive property of God's holiness, God isn't love if he doesn't infinitely punish our sin.

To be holy means to be distinct or set apart from lesser things. Scripture says that there are holy people, places, and things. The priests, temple, and the Scriptures themselves are holy, for they are special and separate from ordinary persons, places, and things. Scripture also says that there are holy actions, for right behavior is superior to wrong choices and good ways are better than bad paths. When Scripture declares that God is holy, it means that he is entirely set apart both in his being and in his actions. He is the wholly other God, who by nature always seeks and does what is best.

God's love requires holiness for the same reason that loving parents put limits on their children. A parent without boundaries may be exceptionally sweet, but no amount of smiles and kind words will make their children feel loved. A pushover parent lacks gravitas, a firm core that stiffens his love into something solid that can support his children. His limp love is like a sagging trampoline. Such a parent's children tremble and shake as they make their way through this world, for there is simply too much give in his sentimental slop to enable them to walk normally.

The easygoing parent fails to love properly because he lacks both components of holiness, holiness of being and of action. He is not behaving as the grown-up, the adult who is supposed to be a cut above the kids, and so he loses the respect of his children. And because he is needy of his children's approval, the parent is unwilling to insist on what is best but merely goes along with whatever his children want. His children may moan and complain, but they won't feel safe until their parent establishes a boundary. A loving parent draws a line in the sand and warns that children who cross it will receive consequences. And then he follows through.

God is not the parent—or Father—of everyone, for reasons I mentioned earlier in this chapter. However, as the Benevolent King of the whole earth, he exercises his love according to the same principles of holiness. The God presented in *Love Wins* doesn't properly love because he lacks both components of holiness. First, he isn't entirely set apart in his being, for Bell implies that a sin against him is not significantly worse than a sin against human people and the earth. Indeed, *Love Wins* rarely speaks about sin in relation to God, and when it does it suggests that he should get over it and not punish people forever for whatever offense he might feel.

Second, he isn't entirely set apart in his actions, for the God in *Love Wins* does not set firm limits on his human creatures. Bell says there is a subjective difference between those who trust and appreciate God's salvation and those who don't, but ultimately both are equally loved and accepted by God. Both are "at the party" regardless of what they believe or how they behave (p. 169). Bell not only erases the spatial boundary between those who are in the family of God and those who are not, but he also removes any temporal boundary that would place a limit on those who haven't yet acknowledged their salvation. Like an insecure king who desperately wants to be loved, the God of *Love Wins* may wring his hands for eternity, waiting and longing for a traitorous rebel to give in and run into his arms. God's failure to establish a hard boundary may initially seem like the loving thing to do, but as any spoiled child can tell you, it ultimately isn't. Children who grow up without boundaries don't feel loved by their parents, and they find it hard to respect them enough to love them back.

Ironically then, the God of *Love Wins* is not as loving as the title suggests. He is not entirely holy, and for that reason his love is more like the squishy indulgence of an overmatched parent than the solid, firm resolve of our infinite God. This kind of indulgent love makes for bad parenting, and it's no way to run the universe. Bell's low view of God's holiness also diminishes God's greatest act of love. If we don't actually deserve hell, then Jesus wasn't doing very much on the cross. He wasn't sacrificing his life in our place, but was merely reaffirming how much God cares. How loving is God really, if he didn't actually do anything to save us?

So God's love requires holiness, and his holiness requires the infinite punishment of our sin (see above, "Do We Deserve Eternal Punishment?"). But why must God inflict that infinite punishment upon us? Jesus' death fully satisfied the requirements of God's justice, so that God could be fully "just and the one who justifies those who have faith in Jesus" (Rom. 4:26). The cross is sufficient to cover the debts of the whole world, so why doesn't God apply that sacrifice to everyone? God would be perfectly just and holy if he led everyone to put their faith in his Son. *Why doesn't our loving and holy God save everyone?*

2. It's a great question, but no one is in a position to ask it. *Love Wins* is unable to ask it, at least in the question's present form, because Bell does not believe that God's justice needs to be satisfied. Bell assumes that we haven't offended God *that* much, and so we don't have debts that need to be forgiven. Jesus didn't die to satisfy the holiness of God, but rather to show us that we have always been God's children and can trust him to bring new life out of death. Bell even speculates that hell may ultimately be empty because of God's general love for humanity, not because our debts were paid on the cross.

The damned who are currently in hell are not able to honestly raise the question, for they don't want to be saved. Sure, they would love to escape their unending torment, but they are unwilling to do the very thing that God requires—to lay down their weapons and submit to God's rule over them. As C. S. Lewis wrote, "There are only two kinds of people in the end: those who say to God, 'Thy will be done,' and those to whom God says, in the end, 'Thy will be done.' All that are in Hell, choose it" (Lewis 1978, p. 72). Lost people can hardly blame God for giving them exactly what they want.

We who are saved aren't in a position to ask the question, for the only reason we are not headed for hell is that God graciously changed our hearts so we would love him. It would be the height of ingratitude to criticize God for not doing for others what he didn't have to do for us. There is only one person who has the right to raise the question of hell, and he did. But Jesus did not receive an answer when he cried from the cross, "My God, my God, why have you forsaken me?" (Matt. 27:46). Although his question went unanswered, Jesus' suffering does offer two further insights.

3. We should not expect to solve this question.

The question of "reconciling" a loving God with the existence of hell directly touches on the two areas that we should never expect to comprehend. As I said in chapter one, every question that involves God or the fall will always end in mystery. And so a question which includes both—"Is God unloving if he punishes forever?"—will be even more unsolvable than most. This may feel like a cop-out, but it's precisely the conclusion that the apostle Paul reached in Romans 9–11. He affirmed that God must be both loving and just in saving Jacob but not Esau, but he could not explain how. He simply praised the wisdom and knowledge of God, whose judgments are unsearchable and whose paths are "beyond tracing out" (Rom. 11:33). If this is the best that Paul can do even as he's writing inspired Scripture, why should we think that our attempts will be able to say more?

4. No one has suffered more from hell than God.
We may not know why God does not save everyone from going to hell, but we do know that God himself experienced it. The Apostles' Creed states that Jesus descended into hell or "descended to the dead" (see McGrath 1998, pp. 59–72). In that eternal moment when the perfect Son was intolerably forsaken by his Father, God himself experienced the worst torments of hell. This does not tell us why God permits hell to exist, but it does assure us that God is love. He may not get everyone out of hell, but for our sake he has allowed hell to get to him. No one will ever suffer more than our loving, infinite God already has. We may rightly wonder why God doesn't empty hell, but we should never raise the question of hell without shuddering even more at the thought of the cross.

How Can We Be Safe?

This question is the pastoral motivation behind *Love Wins*. Bell wants the world to know that they can safely rest in the good hands of God. He argues that God isn't the moral monster who damns people to hell for not believing the right facts about Jesus. Rather, he is a father whose "love cannot be earned, and it cannot be taken away" (p. 187). Unfortunately, because Bell switches out the biblical metaphor of a courtroom for his family analogy, his view actually makes his readers less safe.

Christ Alone

The truth is that we are not God's children simply because we belong to the human race. We are the children of Adam, which means that we have inherited his guilt and corruption. We are part of a fallen species destined for hell, not a perfect species automatically headed for heaven.

And so we stand in God's courtroom, guilty for Adam's sin and for our own, awaiting God's just sentence of condemnation. But before the sentence can be read, the Son of the Judge steps forward and announces that he wishes to be damned to hell in our place. Contrary to Bell, this Son is not rescuing us from his evil Father (p. 182), for it was the Father who sent the Son to save us (John 17:3). Neither is this a bipolar God who loves unrepentant sinners while they are alive and then switches gears at their death into a "cruel, mean, vicious tormenter who would ensure that they had no escape from an endless future of agony" (pp. 173–74). God is just, so he will punish those who die under his wrath. But he lovingly sent his Son to bear his wrath in their place.

However, if we fallen creatures don't accept God's love, either because we think they we are too good to go to hell or because God is too "good" to send us there, then we will learn, too late, that our false assurance of safety is the very thing that has made us unsafe. We are saved, not by pretending we don't need saving, not by hoping that everything will work out well because God couldn't possibly be *that* angry with us, but by repenting of our sin and throwing ourselves upon the mercy of the court. Then we will find that we have a merciful and holy God, an advocate who justly emptied all the wrath our sins deserved, but who in mercy poured it out upon himself.

Conclusion

Love Wins raises many questions about the biblical description of God and his relation to hell. We shouldn't expect to completely solve any of these questions, for they directly touch on God and the fall, the two areas which are guaranteed to end in mystery. However, when we remember that we are the ones on trial rather than God, and when we humbly seek to piece together everything Scripture tells us about our loving God and hell, we find that while we can't solve this puzzle, we can say more than enough to feed our faith.

Most importantly, when we stick close to Scripture we avoid putting our salvation at risk. Besides its reimagining of God, the largest problem with *Love Wins* is that ultimately it changes the biblical meaning of the gospel. This is a serious, life-and-death matter, and I will examine it in my final chapter.

Gospel

10

Subtlety — whose perspective

Florencio Ávalos heard the rumble of falling rocks and saw the cloud of dust billowing toward him. He screamed, then covered his mouth as soot and ash tumbled over his head. The dust hung in the air for hours, plunging the mine shaft into total darkness. Florencio choked out a yell, which was answered by a wheezing reply nearby. He felt his way toward the voice, and slowly, over the next few hours, the thirty-three trapped miners found each other.

Initially their situation seemed hopeless. They were thousands of feet underground, and there was no way to tell if anyone knew where they were, let alone if others would be able to reach them. Florencio's foreman, Luis Urzúa, immediately recognized what needed to be done. He led the men to a secure room and organized them into work units. He gave them jobs, parceled out their meager food supply, and sought to instill a sense of purpose. Days passed, then a week, and then another, with no word from the outside. The men were quickly giving in to despair. Some openly spoke of suicide, while others wondered whether they should cannibalize the first among them to die.

Florencio pulled a faded picture of his wife, Mónica, out of his wallet. His fingers caressed her face. What he wouldn't give to see her just once more! Wait, he thought he heard something! It was a distant, shrill rat-a-tat. Florencio called to the others, and they gathered around, silently praying as the drill bit bore down, slowly but in their general direction. Tap, tap, tap, tap.

The tapping startled Florencio, and he bolted upright in bed. He reached over and touched Mónica, who was sleeping contentedly beside him. The tapping was coming from their bedroom door. Little Mario had awakened from a bad dream, and he was calling for someone to comfort him. Florencio cleared the fog from his head and swung his legs over the edge of the bed. He was sorry his dream had been interrupted, and he told himself that the next time he fell asleep he would try to dream that his work crew had been rescued.

The end of my fictional dream is far less satisfying than the real outcome of the trapped Chilean miners in 2010. In the real story, the drill did find the miners' safe room. The miners were able to send a note up the small auger shaft, telling their families and the world that the crew was alive. Drillers spent the next two months boring a larger hole that could pass a human rescue capsule. Florencio Ávalos was the first miner to step into the claustrophobic rocket and ride up to the surface, and over the next few hours each of his companions followed. Television delivered the inspiring story to the watching and praying world.

A real rescue beats an imaginary rescue every day of the week, because it involves actual risk. An imaginary story may interest us and even draw us in, but it's not nearly as powerful and inspiring as the real thing. It's one thing to pretend that we're drowning or being chased by bad guys; it's entirely different to actually be lost at sea or dodging bullets. Real-life rescues always have the most at stake.

And that's important, because the most engaging stories have something at stake—something that could be won or lost. We identify with characters who must overcome long odds for something worthwhile, especially life over death. We wouldn't pull for the characters, cheering their successes and mourning their failures, if they weren't fighting for something significant which could be irretrievably lost. So as I finish my response to *Love Wins*, I want to ask whether it tells a compelling story. What exactly is at stake in the gospel story of *Love Wins*? And how does it square with an evangelical understanding of the gospel of Jesus Christ?

The Gospel of *Love Wins*

Rob Bell argues that our fundamental human problem is ignorance. We don't know that "the universe is on our side" (p. 137), so we live in fear. Because we're not sure that we're going to be alright, we fight for what we hope will deliver us security and significance in this life or the next. But this just spins our wheels in deeper, and soon we're creating our own minihells as we steal from the weak and lash out at the strong. Bell appreciates that our fear is real, but he contends that there is little real, lasting danger. Why? Because God is good and he has not abandoned us in this world. We are already safe with him; we just don't realize it. We all would be fine if we simply learned "to trust that we are loved and that a new word has been spoken about us, a new story is being told about us" (p. 195).

We need to hear the news that God is in charge and ultimately everything will work out splendidly for every human being who has ever lived, is living, and will live on earth.

To use an analogy, Bell's view suggests that we're like a kindergartner on their first day of school. The child is anxious and fearful. Will they be able to locate their bus to return home safely? Will they make friends and fit in with classmates? What if they get lost in the hallways? The child's parents and older siblings know there is nothing to worry about, but no matter how many times they reassure the child, "You'll be fine," they know that the only way the child is going to learn this truth is by swallowing hard and going to school. Soon the child will look back on the first week of school and wonder why they were ever afraid of something so small and insignificant.

Bell suggests that, like that kindergartner, we humans are never truly in serious danger. Our only problem is unfounded fears which arise from our ignorance that everything is actually fine. So the stakes in Bell's story are extremely low. It would be nice, he presumes, if people discovered here and now that they are in good hands and that death always leads to life, but it's not immediately necessary. If they missed all the cues in creation—the bleak death of winter that inexorably leads to the new life of spring, seeds that die in order to sprout into something even more beautiful, plants and animals sacrificing their lives so we might digest them into the life of our bodies—they should still figure it out in the analogous but more explicit message of Jesus' cross and resurrection. And should they die without ever hearing the gospel of Jesus Christ in this life, they can count on multiple chances to hear and respond in the next one. Even if they are a member of a different faith, God will likely provide for them in due time.

Eventually the mysteries of life and death will be laid out before them. They will see Jesus face-to-face (p. 61), and they will have the clear and definite knowledge of heaven and hell. They could choose death and separation from God if they really wanted, but what would be the point? Bell seems to expect that most if not all will choose life when the options are staring them straight in the face. So everyone starts life already safe with God, and as long as they don't openly curse God and jump permanently into whatever hell is, they will remain safe with God forever.

Whatever the biblical merits of Bell's case—and I think I've shown in this book they're exceedingly slim—his view makes an exceptionally bland story. There is no drama. No deep conflict requiring resolution. No compelling need for a satisfying denouement. Where is the insurmountable problem that must be overcome? Where's the cliff we might fall off? Where's the foreshadowed death that can be avoided only by intervention from the outside? Nothing is ever really at stake in Bell's tale of limitless happy endings. It has even less suspense than a child's bedtime story, whose main goal is to reassure sleepy children that all is right with the world because everyone lived happily ever after.

I appreciate that the looming threat of hell can make us uncomfortable, but if we eliminate this from the Scriptures we deflate the true and even more astonishing biblical story. A world without the real possibility of hell, of eternal death, would increasingly resemble the contrived world of the film The Truman Show, comically and tragically unrealistic. If the cross teaches us anything, it's that this is a wild, dangerous world. If the Son of God can be crucified, then anything is possible here. A world which killed Jesus may well have a large number of murderers headed for hell. The stakes are that high.

Bell's diminished view of hell not only removes the villain from the biblical story; it also eliminates the possibility that God is loving, at least in the biblical sense. Richard Hays rightly argues that "the biblical story teaches us that God's love cannot be reduced to 'inclusiveness,'" but that, rather, "what the New Testament means by 'love' is embodied concretely in the *cross*. As 1 John 3:16 declares with powerful simplicity, 'We know love by this, that he laid down his life for us—and we ought to lay down our lives for one another'" (Hays, p. 202). Scripture states that God's love rescues us from his wrathful punishment on those in hell. If there is no looming threat of wrath and hell, then there is little for God to do except be generally kind to everyone. That may be nice, but the Bible wouldn't say that this God is love.

Even worse, what should we think about a Father who turns his back on his own Son, sending him to an excruciating death that wasn't actually necessary? If the cross doesn't add anything that we couldn't already learn from Jesus' life and ministry, and if Jesus' words and deeds don't tell us anything we couldn't already learn from nature, then forcing Jesus to go to the cross seems to be a genuine case of divine child abuse. To use Bell's own words,

> If there was an earthly father who was like that, we would call the authorities.
> If there was an actual human dad who was that volatile, we would contact child protection services immediately. (p. 174)

It's ironic that the God of *Love Wins* seems to have issues with love. It's doubly ironic that God doesn't even win. He doesn't win because the stakes are so low that there is little for him to win. There are no winner-take-all battles to be fought, no grotesque enemies to be overcome, no abject powers of hell to defeat. The God of *Love Wins* does nothing heroic, for there is no obstacle that calls for heroism. He's good to all, but he's not gracious, because no one desperately needs his grace. He merely hugs the world in his warm embrace, patiently waiting for people to trust his story about them, either in this life or after they die.

Love Wins simply doesn't have enough gospel. The gospel is the "good news that will cause great joy" because "a Savior has been born to you" (Luke 2:10–11). It is not the tepid news that you don't really need saving, that you've never been lost except in your imagination, and that God already accepts you just the way you are. Such "good news" will convince only people who are quite impressed with themselves. Those who recognize the depth of their sin and rebellion will instinctively know that they need more than a hearty reassurance that everything is fine. They will understand that this optimistic message cruelly leaves sinners pretty much where it finds them. The gospel, as Bell likes to say, has to be better than that. And it is.

The Gospel of Jesus

I began this chapter by suggesting that the best stories have something significant at stake. While that is true, the *very* best stories not only have something important at risk; they also end in success. Think of your most memorable sports moments. Weren't they watching your favorite team win a championship? My favorite teams are all in Cleveland, so I'm not speaking from personal experience, but I can imagine it feels good to cheer your own team on to a championship. Their entire season was on the line, and they won! It doesn't get any better than that in the world of sports.

Or consider a riveting story, such as *Les Misérables*. Victor Hugo pulls you into rooting hard for the escaped convict Jean Valjean. You agonize for him as he stays on the lam, avoiding the dogged pursuit of Javert in order to care for his beloved Cosette. Will he stay free long enough to keep his promise to her mother? Will he be able to guide his orphan girl into adulthood? Even though Jean Valjean dies at the end, you cry tears of joy because he married off Cosette to the kind Marius and fulfilled his mission. It's a deeply satisfying ending.

The Bible tells a better story than *Les Misérables*, not only because it's true, but also because in its story everybody and everything in the world is put at risk by the most insurmountable problem. You and I and the fate of everyone who has ever lived hung in the balance. It would take a miracle—a whole series of them actually—to defeat the enemy and provide salvation for the world. And that is precisely what Jesus did.

Hear the Christian gospel: we all are rebellious traitors against God and his kingdom, and for that we are dying now and are destined to suffer forever in the ultimate despair of hell. We are actually God's enemies (not merely in our imagination), and we deserve whatever torment we have coming. Worse, we are entirely unable to lay down our weapons and change sides, for as the apostle Paul reminds us, we are "dead in [our] transgressions and sins...by nature deserving of wrath...without hope and without God in the world" (Eph. 2:1–12). We are unwilling to change, and unable to change our hearts and minds so we would be willing.

God justly could have been content to destroy our insurrection and wipe us from the earth. But he took pity on us, and while "we were God's enemies," "while we were still sinners, Christ died for us" (Rom. 5:8, 10). The cross is a most unusual weapon of choice, but the death of his beloved Son was the only way that God could defeat our sin and death. Satan had become the functional ruler of us and of this world when he tempted Adam and Eve, God's appointed rulers of creation, to switch their allegiance to him. Now a Son of Adam, the Son of God, had come to earth to win us back.

Jesus did not conquer Satan in some heavy-handed way, using his overwhelming force to throw him down. God beat Satan on a level playing field. He became a creature, vulnerable to Satan's attacks, and defeated the devil through weakness rather than shock and awe. In this way he did not so much overpower Satan as outwit him. He showed Satan and his demons to be fools, for, "having disarmed the powers and authorities, he made a public spectacle of them, triumphing over them by the cross" (Col. 2:15).

Demons shrieked and danced around the cross, deliriously surprised by how easily Jesus had fallen into their trap. What they didn't realize was that they had walked straight into his. Jesus knew what C. S. Lewis—in *The Lion, the Witch and the Wardrobe*—called the "magic deeper still," that "when a willing victim who had committed no treachery was killed in a traitor's stead, the Table would crack and Death itself would start working backward" (see Hooper 1998, p. 439). Death died in the death of Christ, for Jesus bore our penalty in our place. Jesus took our sin and death down with him into the grave, and when he arose he left them in the dust. Paul explains, "He was delivered over to death for our sins and was raised to life for our justification" (Rom. 4:25). Jesus' spectacular resurrection is not merely an authoritative illustration of a general truth that is embedded in creation. Rather it is the turning point of world history, for that is the moment that God reversed the curse, releasing forever those who put their faith in Jesus. Jesus' death and resurrection don't merely *reveal* that death leads to life; they are the very things that *make it true.* Jesus triumphed over sin, death, and Satan by his cross and empty tomb, and anyone who trusts his finished work alone will join his victory.

Last Questions

As I mentioned in chapter one, Scripture repeatedly claims that we need to trust in Jesus to receive the benefits of his victory (John 3:18, 36; 6:29; Acts 4:12; 10:43; 16:30–31; Rom. 10:13–15). This causes some people to ask, "Do people go to hell simply because they didn't believe in Jesus?" And, "Is the difference between the saved and the damned simply that one group believed the right set of facts and the other didn't?"

The answer to both questions is no. First, the Bible says that people are destined for hell because they're sinners. There are many who tragically die without ever hearing the gospel of Christ. God would not punish them for what they never heard, but he will hold them accountable for what they did know. Scripture declares that everyone has some knowledge of God because they are made in God's image and they live in God's world, but, left to themselves, they "suppress the truth by their wickedness…so that [they] are without excuse" (Rom. 1:18–20). No one can accuse God of unjustly sending them to hell, for while they didn't have as much light as others are blessed to receive, they did sinfully distort and push aside whatever knowledge of God they had.

Second, the everlasting difference between Christians and non-Christians is not merely mental—one group possessed a set of facts that the other didn't—but that the members of one group are born again and those of the other are not. Beliefs play an important role, because as Jesus told Nicodemus, the Spirit uses the truth about Jesus to regenerate sinners (John 3:1–18), and as Paul explained, it's impossible to call on Jesus if you have never even heard of him (Rom. 10:9–15). But gospel proclamation is merely the means God uses to bring new life, and it's this new life that makes the difference.

Paul exclaims, "Therefore, if anyone is in Christ, that person is a new creation; the old has gone, the new is here!" (2 Cor. 5:17). And how does someone come to be "a new creation in Christ"? Paul says it's by hearing and receiving God's message of reconciliation. This is why Paul committed his life to spreading the good news of God's love. He writes, "We are therefore Christ's ambassadors, as though God were making his appeal through us. We implore you on Christ's behalf: Be reconciled to God" (2 Cor. 5:20).

One final question is whether evangelical Christians are entirely consistent in their belief that sinners must believe in Jesus to be saved. If we claim that God saves our deceased infants, who never put their faith in Christ, then why won't we say that he also extends grace to adults who have never heard? This is a perceptive question, and it reminds us that we must be careful as we comfort grieving parents. We must not make promises that God himself has not made, but neither should we shrug and say we have no idea where their child is. We do know that our loving and just Father loves our children even more than we do, and Scripture does suggest that he has a special relationship with the children of believers (1 Cor. 7:14). So while we must be careful not to speak with certainty, we may follow the lead of the Synod of Dordt, which, because of its robust belief in divine sovereignty, said that "godly parents ought not to doubt the election and salvation of their children whom God calls out of this life in infancy" (see *Canons of Dordt*, first point, art. 17).

Unlike the case of young children, the fate of rationally capable people who never put their faith in Jesus is often addressed in the Bible. We may wish God would grant these people a chance to hear and respond when they die, but we can't say we hope for that, because the warnings of Scripture run hard in the other direction. We read repeatedly that people who die in their sin will suffer forever in hell, and the only way to escape such a fate is to believe in Jesus. This fact is so well assumed in Scripture that it comes out even when the author isn't trying to make the point. Consider Paul's protest against the Jews in 1 Thessalonians 2:15–16. He complains that "they displease God and are hostile to everyone in their effort to keep us from *speaking to the Gentiles so that they may be saved*" (italics added). Paul doesn't mean for this to be a salvation text, but notice that he assumes that if he doesn't speak the gospel to the Gentiles then they won't be saved. This explains why Paul risked and ultimately lost his life for the sake of the gospel. He knew that the good news he had wasn't merely something that would be nice for others to know. He believed that it was absolutely necessary if they were going to be saved.

Conclusion

We are not saved by the universal fatherhood of God or by a cosmic Christ who has written the general principles of life in nature. We are saved by Jesus Christ, our Redeemer King, who in history's greatest and truest story defeated the powers of hell when he died for our sin and rose again. We are saved by this Jesus, and him alone.

Since Jesus is God, and God is love, we may say that love has won. It won at the cross and the empty tomb, and it will win completely when our victorious King returns. Jesus will bring history to its climax, and he will live forever with his people in the everlasting joys of the new earth. Those who are not prepared for his return will perish forever, and so love must also warn. Why would you resist his love? Why risk everlasting torment in hell? God's love has won, and so can you. Only repent and believe—in Christ alone.

ODD statmnt for Calvinist. Ha!

Afterword

Our beliefs about heaven and hell are extremely important, for what we think about them has major implications for our view of Scripture, God, humanity, sin, Jesus, the cross and resurrection, and the gospel itself. As I have demonstrated in this book, when we divert from the church's traditional, biblical understanding of heaven and hell, we ultimately end up with an entirely new version of the Christian faith.

These issues are too important to obscure by giving attention to news media stories that tend to focus on personalities rather than substance; we must resist such distractions. Whenever these kinds of deeply biblical and theological issues surface in the church, both sides have good people who earnestly desire to serve Jesus and the kingdom. It's important for us all to remain loving and respectful even as we might disagree. Disagreements don't have to become personality attacks and rumor mongering. Disagreements can be opportunities to clarify what we believe and what the Bible actually says. I hope that this book will contribute toward such clarifications.

Christ Alone

These issues are too important to resolve on the basis of one writer's thoughts. It ultimately doesn't matter what any of us thinks about these matters, but only what God says about them. Please get together with a group of friends, take out your Bibles, and study these issues for yourselves. Go to the book website and you will find discussion questions to aid your study. The Scriptures do tell us about heaven, hell, and the fate of everyone who has ever lived. If you are open to whatever you may find there, I think you'll discover that the gospel is better—dangerously better—than anything you have ever imagined. Blessings to you on your journey of faith.

Mike Wittmer

book resources: www.christalone.com
my blog: www.michaelwittmer.net

Sources

Alcorn, Randy. *Heaven*. Carol Stream, IL: Tyndale House, 2004.

Anselm of Canterbury. *Why God Became Man*. In *Anselm of Canterbury: The Major Works*. Edited by Brian Davies and G. R. Evans. New York: Oxford Unversity Press, 2008.

Augustine. *Confessions*. Translated by Henry Chadwick. New York: Oxford University Press, 1991.

———. "On Nature and Grace." In *Answer to the Pelagians*, translated by Roland J. Teske, part 1, pp. 217–268. *The Works of Saint Augustine: A Translation for the 21st Century*, vol. 23. Hyde Park, NY: New City Press, 1997.

Augustyn, Adam, ed. *American Literature from 1600 through the 1850s*. New York: Rosen Educational Services, 2010.

Barth, Karl. *Church Dogmatics*. Vol. 2, part 2. Translated by G. W. Bromiley. Edinburgh: T. & T. Clark, 1957.

Bell, Rob. *Love Wins: A Book About Heaven, Hell and the Fate of Every Person Who Ever Lived*. New York: Harper One, 2011.

Bierma, Nathan. *Bringing Heaven Down to Earth*. Phillipsburg, NJ: Presbyterian & Reformed, 2005.

Channing, William E. "Unitarian Christianity." In *The Works of William E. Channing*. 2 vols. in 1. 1882. Reprint, New York: Burt Franklin, 1970.

Edwards, Jonathan. "Sinners in the Hands of an Angry God."
In *A Jonathan Edwards Reader*, edited by John E. Smith,
Harry S. Stout, and Kenneth P. Minkema, pp. 89–105.
New Haven: Yale University Press, 1995.

Erickson, Millard. *Christian Theology*. Edited by L. Arnold
Hustad. 2nd ed. Grand Rapids: Baker Academic, 2001.

Galli, Mark. "What's Up with Hell?" *Christianity Today*, April
2011, 63–65.

Hays, Richard. *Moral Vision of the New Testament*. San Francisco: Harper Collins, 1996.

Hesselink, I. John. *Calvin's First Catechism: A Commentary*. Lou-
isville: Westminster John Knox, 1997.

Hooper, Walter. *C.S. Lewis: A Complete Guide to His Life &
Works*. New York: HarperOne, 1998.

Lewis, C. S. *The Great Divorce*. New York: Macmillan, 1946.
Reprint, 1978.

———. *Letters to Malcolm: Chiefly on Prayer*. New York: Mariner
Books, 2002.

Luther, Martin. "The Bondage of the Will." In *Martin Luther's
Basic Theological Writings*. Edited by Timothy F. Lull. 2nd
ed. Minneapolis: Fortress Press, 2005.

———. "Letter to Hans von Rechenberg." In *Luther's Works* 43,
edited and translated by G. Wienke and H. T. Lehmann.
Philadelphia: Fortress Press, 1968.

McGrath, Alister E. *The Christian Theology Reader*. 3rd ed.
Malden, MA: Blackwell, 2007.

———. *"I Believe": Exploring the Apostles' Creed*. Downers Grove,
IL: InterVarsity, 1998.

Niebuhr, H. Richard. *The Kingdom of God in America*. 1937.
Reprint, New York: Harper & Bros., 1959.

———. *Radical Monotheism and Western Culture*. New York:
Harper and Row, 1970.

Plantinga, Cornelius, Jr. *Engaging God's World*. Grand Rapids:
Eerdmans, 2002.

———. *Not the Way It's Supposed to Be: A Breviary of Sin*. Grand
Rapids: Eerdmans, 1995.

Prothero, Stephen. *God is Not One: The Eight Rival Religions that Run the World—and Why Their Differences Matter.* New York: HarperOne, 2010.

Rahner, Karl. *Theological Investigations.* Vol. 14, *Ecclesiology, Questions in the Church, the Church in the World.* Translated by David Bourke. London: Darton, Longman and Todd, 1976.

Schleiermacher, Friedrich. *The Christian Faith.* Edited by Hugh Ross Mackintosh and James Stuart Stewart. Vol. 1. New York: Continuum, 1999.

Spurgeon, Charles Haddon. *Spurgeon at His Best.* Edited by Tom Carter. Grand Rapids: Baker, 1991.

Stevenson, James, ed. *Creeds, Councils, and Controversies: Documents Illustrating the History of the Church, A.D. 337–461.* London: SPCK, 1989.

Tillich, Paul. *Systematic Theology.* Chicago: University of Chicago Press, 1957.

Torrance, Thomas. *Karl Barth: An Introduction to His Early Theology, 1910-1931.* New York: Harper & Row, 1962

Truss, Lynne. *Eats, Shoots & Leaves: The Zero Tolerance Approach to Punctuation.* New York: Gotham, 2004.

Vande Bunte, Matt. "Selling Books on Sunday." *Grand Rapids Press*, April 4, 2011, A1–A2.

Warren, Rick. *The Purpose Driven Life.* Grand Rapids: Zondervan, 2002.

Wright, N. T. *Surprised by Hope.* San Francisco: HarperOne, 2008.